THE COMMUNICATION SCARCITY IN AGRICULTURE

Today, the general public craves information on food and agriculture with an unprecedented passion. But the agricultural sector, unaccustomed to an interested and inquisitive society, has largely failed to respond to the public's demands for information. Instead, corporations, time-pressed journalists, bloggers, media celebrities, film-makers, authors, and concerned consumers jumped in to fill the void. Food is emotional, and these players – some well-intentioned and others not – got a lot of traction playing off consumer fears of the unknown.

This critical and timely book explains how changing demographics, cultural shifts, technological advances, and agriculture's silence all combined to create the perfect storm – a great chasm between those who know, and those who don't know, agriculture. The ramifications of a poorly informed consumer base are now becoming clear in our policy debates and consumer-driven business decisions. There is a lot of common ground between the agricultural sector and its consumer base, but each group largely fails to appreciate it, and the consequences of such a divide grow increasingly dire.

Drawing on a wide range of expertise, from leading agricultural researchers to major agribusiness leaders to consumer advocates,

Eise and Hodde lay out exactly why communication is so urgently critical to our modern-day agricultural system. They outline the major themes affecting agricultural communication – perception, emotion, technology, science – and what we can do *now* to improve the debate and safeguard our future food supply for generations to come. This book is suitable for those who study agriculture, environmental economics, and mass media and communication.

Jessica Eise is the Director of Communications in the Agricultural Economics Department at Purdue University, where she also teaches. She has a master's in Journalism and International Relations from New York University. Eise worked internationally in communications for five years before a stint in Washington, DC, in policy communications.

Whitney Hodde is a Research Assistant in the Agricultural Economics Department at Purdue University. She has a master's in Agricultural Economics from Purdue University. She was raised on a farm in Iowa and worked in Washington, DC, for seven years as an environmental finance expert in the non-profit world.

THE COMMUNICATION SCARCITY IN AGRICULTURE

Jessica Eise and Whitney Hodde

LONDON AND NEW YORK

First published 2017
by Routledge
2 Park Square, Milton Park, Abingdon, Oxon OX14 4RN

and by Routledge
711 Third Avenue, New York, NY 10017

Routledge is an imprint of the Taylor & Francis Group, an informa business

British Library Cataloguing in Publication Data
A catalogue record for this book is available from the British Library

Library of Congress Cataloging in Publication Data
Names: Eise, Jessica, author. | Hodde, Whitney, author.
Title: The communication scarcity in agriculture / Jessica Eise and
Whitney Hodde.
Description: New York, NY : Routledge, 2016.
Identifiers: LCCN 2016007719| ISBN 9781138650602 (hardback) |
ISBN 9781138650619 (pbk.) | ISBN 9781315625201 (ebook)
Subjects: LCSH: Communication in agriculture.
Classification: LCC S494.5.C6 E37 2016 | DDC 630.1/4--dc23
LC record available at http://lccn.loc.gov/2016007719

ISBN: 978-1-138-65060-2 (hbk)
ISBN: 978-1-138-65061-9 (pbk)
ISBN: 978-1-315-62520-1 (ebk)

Typeset in Bembo
by Saxon Graphics Ltd, Derby

To Dr. Ken Foster for his unwavering support, without which this book would never have been written. To Drs. Wally Tyner, Allan Gray, Otto Doering, Chris Hurt, and the myriad of other professors who inspired us, encouraged us and guided us. Lastly, to every person who gave generously of their time and knowledge so that we could create this manuscript – one which could never have been written alone.

CONTENTS

FOREWORD

by Dr. Robert Paarlberg

This new book fills an important gap. There are already plenty of books to read covering today's polarized debate over food and farming (my own book *Food Politics: What Everyone Needs to Know* is one such summary). But we have not had, until now, a look at this problem through the eyes of an experienced media professional situated inside an elite school of agriculture. In *The Communication Scarcity in Agriculture*, Jessica Eise at Purdue University and her co-author Whitney Hodde dissect the current culture war over food and farming from a vantage point sympathetic to commercial farming yet disciplined by academic rigor.

Eise and Hodde see the communication problem clearly. For the first time in history, in rich countries such as the United States, commercial farming is something almost nobody encounters first hand. Farm and ranch families now make up only about 2 percent of our population. In some parts of the country, including New England where I live, young people who become interested in agriculture – and there are now quite a few – have no direct access to the modern farming operations of the Midwest, or Florida, or California, where most of our nation's food is grown. They can only visit or work on the tiny local farms found in the region, but most of these are part-time, antique operations geared to making direct sales to local communities through seasonal farmers markets. This is a fascinating niche, but less than 2 percent of America's fresh produce is actually grown and sold this way.

The only knowledge these young people have about larger commercial farms comes from the media, or online, or from what they hear in conversations with friends. Media coverage of American agriculture, at least outside of the nation's farming heartland, is seldom well informed and frequently hostile.

Eise and Hodde want to change this reality by reminding non-agricultural readers to think more carefully about where their information is coming from, and by encouraging agriculturalists – including farmers, agricultural scientists, and other academics – to view more effective communication as a serious professional responsibility. This will mean engaging more frequently with those that do not share their views. It will mean mastering the facts, listening more carefully to the concerns of others, and then speaking and writing using words and concepts others can understand. It does not mean lashing out at those who hold poorly informed views, or denigrating the character of critics, or retreating into smug silence.

Does this sound easy? Eise and Hodde know it is not. From personal experience I know it is not. That's why good communication about agriculture remains so scarce. This new book will be valued for the timely assistance it provides in overcoming the deficit.

Dr. Robert Paarlberg
Adjunct Professor of Public Policy, Harvard Kennedy School

FOREWORD

by Dr. Sonny Ramaswamy

We live in an era of information overload. The average American takes in a staggering amount of information per day – over 34 gigabytes. Yet even with the vast amount of knowledge at our fingertips, the United States of America is one of the most scientifically illiterate countries, particularly when it comes to food and agriculture. Such scientific illiteracy impedes our progress as a nation, preventing our citizens from demanding policies from their representatives that best represent their interests, and ultimately prevents the informed dialogue needed to address societal challenges. Our debates continue to cycle endlessly around contention, mistrust, and suspicion.

In the face of the changing world, effective and productive communication around food and agriculture will be critical to ensuring the safety of our world's food supply. In *The Communication Scarcity in Agriculture*, Jessica Eise and Whitney Hodde address this head-on. They manage a tricky task by breaking down a broad topic full of multiple players and effectively synthesizing this information into a readable, understandable, and accurate portrayal of what our agricultural communications playing field looks like today.

I spend much of my time addressing the importance of communication in agriculture. This is a priority for me, because, like Eise and Hodde, I understand its critical importance in our nation today. Agriculture, to the public, seems covered in a shroud of secrecy. Agricultural researchers, educators, and stakeholders have historically treated communication as an afterthought, and without their voices speaking up, the conversation has been hijacked by the vocal minority. These individuals span both sides of the political spectrum – from the Food Babe (Vani Hari) and her pseudoscience food claims to Rush Limbaugh, a fomenter of mistrust in science and an avid denier of some of the most pressing challenges to our world.

Studies by the Pew Research Center show that where almost 90 percent of the scientific community views genetically engineered crops as safe, only approximately 40 percent of the general public believes the same. If they aren't listening to the scientific community, where are they getting their information from? Media, in all forms, has become the overbearing voice on all subjects. From the constant stream of news outlets, to the never-ending barrage of social media posts, it's physically impossible to escape this relentless stream of information. When the media present these controversial issues, scientific research is often presented side by side with the counter-argument of a celebrity, famous person, or "expert" with no credentials on the topic at hand. More often than not, the focus and trusted viewpoint are that of the famous person, not the scientific evidence. Recently, George Mason University and Yale University researchers have shown, as with the spike of believers in climate change after Pope Francis's speech about it, that people are more willing to believe information from someone they trust. Establishing trust, understanding perceptions, and crafting messages that resonate by *listening* to the real concerns of consumers and the public is a cornerstone of this book.

The public understandably have angst and feel disempowered about the food they and their families consume. The conundrum for agricultural scientists is that while the average American loves the latest technology in their smartphones and hand-held devices, they are less likely to be accepting of technologies such as genetic modification of their food, because food is ingested; interestingly, however, the same public willingly accept drugs and medications derived from genetic engineering. Simply throwing data at a mistrustful public about the safety of genetically engineered food does not mitigate the angst; and rather than reacting to pseudoscientific information, it's critically important for agricultural scientists to proactively frame the information in a manner that promotes understanding and allays apprehension, so that the public are helped to make informed decisions about the complex issues around food.

To improve our agricultural communications, we need to, as Eise and Hodde write, turn up the volume on science. Many grants and programs are aimed not only at advancing agriculture, but also at forwarding the conversations pertaining to it. These conversations, however, can't just happen at a national level. By utilizing the extension system, present in the 3,143 counties and county-equivalents in the United States, information can be spread to residents across the United States. Extension can work more on translating the information land grant colleges have gained through their research into understandable language for those within their communities – and they can *be that trusted voice* on polarizing, contentious issues.

This book is a good place to start. Eise and Hodde address how we as agriculturalists can become more effective communicators, and how the public themselves can become better informed. They present a reorientation approach, combining the perspectives of agriculture's five biggest players: consumers, farmers, agribusinesses, policymakers, and the academic researchers and extensionists. Reorienting an ingrained culture will take time, but this book is one of the first steps towards getting rid of agriculture's "shroud of secrecy" and breaking through the information overload to deliver agriculture's story to the public at large.

Dr. Sonny Ramaswamy

PREFACE

Today's communication environment

Many of the greatest challenges confronting our food and agricultural dialogue are a result of the revolutionizing changes that have swept our communication environment. The agricultural sector is not alone in facing this rapidly evolving terrain. All industries have confronted this task and must contend with a completely new way of receiving and distributing information. For agriculture, there is an additional pressure that compounds the situation. Technological advances have also radically reduced the percentage of Americans working in agriculture, leaving many consumers far removed and unaware of how our food is produced.[1] Only a couple of generations ago, almost everyone knew someone in agriculture. You don't need to work very hard on communicating an issue when everyone is coming from a shared background. Today, however, few consumers know someone who works in agriculture.

When considering the current communication climate, there are three key elements to understand that will contextualize many of the challenges: the mobile mind shift, changes in traditional journalism and the loss of information curation with the advent of the internet. These matters are periodically discussed, yet to fully internalize them requires a new mindset. This is one of the reasons why it is so challenging to understand and adapt to this environment. Changing a mindset requires constant diligence.

"We have learned that anything we need will be available anywhere, at any time, on our smartphones ... The result of this accumulated experience with mobile apps is that our minds have shifted. Not only can we *do new things*. We now also *expect new things*," write the authors of *The Mobile Mind Shift*. They define the 'mobile mind shift' as a dramatic change in how we perceive our reality: the expectation that you can get what you want in your immediate context and moments of need.[2]

Not much sounds less compatible with the realities of agriculture than that mindset. It is almost absurd how grossly misaligned 'instant satisfaction' is when juxtaposed against the biological reality of growing food. Yet the two *are not* mutually exclusive. As we dig into later in the book, effective communication around agricultural issues can happen in this environment.

In practical terms, the mobile mind shift increases the need for responsiveness and transparency. Rumors and speculation don't just 'blow over' anymore. People don't want answers, they expect them. This requires a shift from defensive communications to offensive communications. Anticipating what communication issues will arise and getting ahead of them is key. Flying by the seat of your pants or expecting something negative to go away is no longer an effective communication strategy in today's world.

The second element to consider is the shift away from traditional journalism. Newspaper ad revenues from digital and print media for newspapers are nearly a third of what they were in 2003 and newsroom employment continues its downward trend.[3] There are fewer reporters than there once were. This makes fact-checking and careful research much more challenging when working under a deadline. With ad revenues down, digital and print media feel the push to publish what will gain readership – and raise their revenues. More readers are accessing their news through their mobile devices, and mobile readers don't spend as much time reading the news as desktop visitors.[4]

Combine diminished levels of journalists with the demands brought on by a 24-hour news cycle, and, in the words of Pulitzer

Prize-winner Howard Rosenburg, "We have before us bloggers whipping up hyperbole like meringue, and hyperventilating news anchors, ad-libbing reporters, instant nonexperts and hair-trigger pundits shooting from the hip with bombast blazing."[5] Media frenzies are easy to understand in this context.

"At a recent lunch," wrote Donald Kennedy, editor-in-chief of *Science* and former Commissioner of the US Food and Drug Administration, "I asked Phil Taubman, an old friend who has had a distinguished career at the *New York Times*, what he would say about the future of respected daily papers like his that are made by printing with ink in newsprint. Phil suggested that he wasn't sure they had a future. Neither am I." Kennedy goes on to write about his concern that the news crisis has the potential to undermine public understanding of science, which is, more so than at any other time within memory, vitally important to outcomes in regulatory decisions and in shaping a proper relationship with science. What has changed, explained Kennedy in his article, is that "the supply of news and information is widely distributed and has become a public good, without significant barriers to entry."[6]

Kennedy's mention of the 'barriers to entry' refers to the third element of modern communication that is important to understand – the lack of information curation. The internet has ushered in a new era of how we receive and exchange data. Journalists were traditionally known as the gatekeepers. Their role, as defined by society, was to carefully sift through the events of the time, select newsworthy items, and then strive to create a balanced, straightforward portrayal of the facts. Information that was published was held to a certain standard. Despite budget cuts in newsrooms, the same largely holds true today – for journalists. Yet for bloggers, celebrities, talk show hosts, radio stars, YouTube phenomena, and anyone with a social media account, the only barrier to entry is an internet connection.

We've all heard the tongue-in-cheek joke, "If it's on the internet, then it must be true!" The humor is, of course, that anyone can post anything they want on the internet at any time. It can be as fantastical, or as authentic, as any one user pleases. Apart from credible news sites, there is precious little information curation on the internet. It is true that libraries, educational institutions, and unique platforms like Wikipedia all attempt to curate information – but only that which they directly generate. The rate of 'information' generation has outpaced the ability of any entity to validate or invalidate what is being created. Companies, social media divas and the litany of other voices are not held accountable to any of those standards. They can portray any issue they want to their advantage, or the advantage of whomever they please.

These three changes – the mobile mind shift, the move away from traditional journalism, and the advent of the internet and the loss of curated information – are a lot to process. The new world of communications feels unsteady and impossible to navigate. However, the worst option is to be overwhelmed and opt to hide and ignore. The new communication climate is a 'problem' like any other we face in our lives. It can be broken down and approached in small, manageable steps. The five players in agricultural communication – consumers, farmers, policymakers, scientists, and agribusiness – will each have unique ways to approach this. However, there is one unifying requirement for success that applies across the board – active participation.

Notes

1   "USDA ERS – The 20th Century Transformation of U.S. Agriculture and Farm Policy." USDA ERS – The 20th Century Transformation of U.S. Agriculture and Farm Policy. Web. 4 August 2015.
2   T. Schadler, J. Bernoff, and J. Ask, J. (2014) *The Mobile Mind Shift: Engineer Your Business to Win in the Mobile Moment*, Groundswell Press.
3   "Newspapers: Fact Sheet." *Pew Research Centers Journalism Project RSS.* 29 April 2015. Web. 10 August 2015. http://www.journalism. org/2015/04/29/newspapers-fact-sheet/.
4   "State of the News Media 2015" (2015, April 29) Retrieved October 23, 2015, from http://www.journalism.org/2015/04/29/state-of-the-news-media-2015/.
5   H. Rosenberg and C. S. Feldman (2008) *No Time to Think: The Menace of Media Speed and the 24-Hour News Cycle*, A&C Black.
6   Donald Kennedy (2010) "The Future of Science News," *Daedalus* 139(2): 57–65.

ACKNOWLEDGMENTS

The seeds of this book were planted in the chill of early winter 2015 in the graduate course 'Communication and Multimedia in Agricultural Economics.' Those students, Molly Van Dop, Toba Omotilewa and Yian Li, were the launch pads for many great conversations and takes on communication in agriculture. A special thanks to Yuhang Liu for first finding the example of egg prices in California, and to Elizabeth Lunik for being excited enough to participate completely voluntarily despite her workload. An additional thanks to Dan Fladager.

Lastly, we'd like to thank everyone who believed in this project – our delightful editor Andy Humphries and his endlessly cheerful editorial assistant Laura Johnson, our beloved families, and every single person who graciously answered emails, phone calls, and questions without complaint and with endless goodwill. In particular, we would like to offer a big thanks to the Department of Agricultural Economics at Purdue University. Being surrounded by such excellent scholarship and research is a constant source of inspiration.

INTRODUCTION

The scarcity of communication

This book is not our own. It is an accumulation of knowledge from many of the greatest minds in the field. From exceptional academics, agribusiness leaders, farmers, consumer advocates all the way to senators and lobbyists, the combined agricultural expertise of the generous people who have contributed (through interviews, answered emails, and endless patience) can be counted in centuries. A significant number of our interviewees have spent decades if not their entire careers committed to food and agriculture. They have witnessed firsthand the evolution of how we discuss and address critical issues in this field.

With only a cursory glance at this title, one might argue that there is no shortage of discussions about agriculture and our food system these days. If you look deeper, however, there is a dearth of meaningful conversation between the right people. Consumers face challenges in gathering neutral, factual answers to questions and concerns. Many want to better understand the connection between agriculture and our environment, health and future. Yet they are frequently inundated by the imploring voices of social media and marketers while the experienced farmers, scientists and agriculture professionals appear relatively quiet.

To reiterate what has been said so many times before, we have entered into a time of political polarization. This polarization has spilled over into many of our important debates and conversations. One area that has not escaped the poisonous touch of gross polarization is food and agriculture. This is a field that is far too complex, too critical, and simply too important to be allowed to fall victim to this form of contention.

For a long time, people were content so long as food was abundant and affordable. These past twenty years have seen a shift. For the first time in history, a large swath of the population has begun to question where their food comes from. They want it to reflect their ideological values, so they seek to discover the origin of their purchases and whether they are worthy of consumption. This was a massive shift for those working in agriculture, most of whom were largely unprepared for a public voraciously seeking information on issues that had previously been considered too boring or irrelevant to consider.

While the United States boasts some of the best academic agricultural research in the world, these are neutral sources – and rightly so. Yet in being neutral, they are often overwhelmed by glamorous and entertaining messages that strike an emotional chord with consumers. This poses a challenge as the issues that surround agriculture are interconnected and have long, complicated histories; histories that can't be contained in a tweet or a soundbite.

Consumers often pick up these soundbites or solitary articles that boil an issue down to a single sentence or sweeping generalization. This provokes a gut response, a reaction that wouldn't occur if presented with the full argument as opposed to these decontextualized examples. One piece of extreme evidence, taken out of context or misrepresented, provokes uncertainty and fear. This is occurring as consumer voices are gaining market power by asking businesses to give them what they want, or don't want, through support of new regulations and standards. This is a consumer right – even if the consumer doesn't fully understand the history, science, or relational context.

The tentative idea of this book started with, naturally, the observation that there was a problem. The real motive came when we discovered that very little large-scale conceptualization has been formally conducted. As in so many cases, a veritable wealth of knowledge exists, but so much of it is wedged into microcosms of expertise: academic, political, scientific, and others.

To get our fingers on the pulse of the problem, we started with a very simple question: what are some of the biggest problems we face in the communication that surrounds food and agriculture? The answers were poignant, powerful, concerned, and insightful. The themes in responses were often startling in their similarities. But the overarching sentiment by far was one of concern – concern that we aren't doing enough, and concern about the ramifications of our inability to seek common ground.

Based on these overarching themes that emerged in our interviews, research, and observations, we outlined our book. The challenging part of a process like this isn't finding the information, but organizing it and contextualizing it. We've attempted to construct the forest, sometimes not even just from trees, but a stick and a twig at a time. The dialogue surrounding food and agriculture is diverse and pieced together by many different groups that often don't speak inter-disciplinarily: farmers, agribusiness, policymakers, researchers, and consumers. There are a lot of voices to understand and piece together in a consumable way. We have interviewed extensively to collect a broad base of diverse perspectives, yet we acknowledge that our farmer and agribusiness interviewees tend to be weighted towards production agriculture. Despite this, we have consciously strived for a levelheaded and informative approach that respects all production styles and their views.

One of our most alarming finds was that many of the key players in agriculture, those with the most important and credible things to add, simply don't actively join the conversation. These individuals, the people from whom reasoned and experienced opinions could be had, are mostly focused on other things: keeping up with the latest technologies, discussing how to produce more with less, preparing to feed a world of nine billion people, staying competitive. They lack the incentive to focus on communication, particularly as communication in this realm is hard, often uncomfortable, emotional, and most certainly time-consuming.

Despite it being unreasonable to ask someone to put him- or herself into a position of discomfort without incentive, we continue to do so. And somehow, we are perpetually surprised when the results disappoint us. Consequently, many conversations aren't fully informed because they are between like-minded people who are focused on reaffirming their views.

Those in agriculture valiant enough to try and communicate often find it difficult to make any meaningful headway. It would be easy to blame consumers in this case – easy, but not accurate. They don't have a reliable forum from which to garner a well-reasoned conclusion. Consumers do what they can to learn about agriculture and how their food systems work. It's a fashionable topic. They pick up waves of information from the media, celebrities, marketers, political debates, and advocates. These are outlets that aren't always concerned with presenting the whole truth or speaking from a place of thoughtfulness or compassion. As consumers learn about the 'horrors' of conventional agriculture, and agriculture learns about the 'food-crazed' consumer, we begin to view ourselves as fundamentally different human beings. We chuckle (or grumble) a little at the 'other side's' ignorance, and neither recognizes this behavior as ugly or counterproductive. Instead, we walk away from the latest soundbite with our personal worldview reinforced.

When trying to communicate, to view ourselves as fundamentally different from another player is more than just a problem. It's toxic. And it's important to remember that every one of us is guilty of this at one point or another, including your authors. There were many moments of personal realization towards our own behaviors as we wrote this book, and there will surely be many more in the future. We've all been trained to deprecate the other's argument and feelings. It's a knee-jerk reaction in a reactionary political climate: there always needs to be somebody on the other side of the table to yell at, otherwise we don't know how to get our point across.

To undermine communication, belittle it or to ignore it would be reflective of our actions to date. Yet if we continue business as usual, we risk making – or exacerbating – decisions that aren't fully informed or are dominated by emotion and a limited portfolio of the relevant facts. The consequences of an information void and misinformation will become increasingly evident in poor policy decisions and misguided consumer-driven corporate decisions. Creating an awareness and understanding of the problems that lead to such an extreme perspective, and a better understanding of how current information channels and incentives encourage and exacerbate this, is precisely the purpose of this book.

Contention around agricultural issues is not new. New approaches and innovations have brought controversy and discomfort to public discussions before. Embarking into new and unknown territory will always be difficult, and as we continue to work on decreasing hunger, improving health, and adjusting to changes in the climate, it will be necessary. Robert Bakewell, now famous as the pioneer of selective breeding practices during the British Agricultural Revolution in the eighteenth century, faced considerable controversy. His idea, now commonly employed and unquestioned, was to select animals with desirable traits (biggest, healthiest, etc.) and breed them. After fifteen years of this practice, his average lamb increased in size from 22 pounds to 38–40 pounds. For his efforts, Bakewell was denounced from religious pulpits all over England for 'playing God.'

We live in a time far different from Bakewell's eighteenth-century England, but human responses to the unknown remain the same. Technological and societal shifts have changed business models in agriculture. New knowledge and awareness of environmental issues have provoked state and local governments, conservation programs, extension agents, and farmers to adapt and respond. Yet with all of the great and new innovations in agriculture, poor communications placed consumers in a vulnerable position where it is only too easy to misinterpret reality or succumb to fear-inducing snippets of 'information.'

Communications in agriculture is a difficult topic to tackle because agriculture itself is such a broad field. There are many different players filling many different roles and receiving information from a wide array of sources. We recognize that it would be naive, even hypocritical, to suggest that we could aggregate and consequently convey all of the economic, behavioral, and other scientific truths that underlie the many complex communications issues in agriculture. If we were to strive to this extremely high and elusive bar, this book would come out about a decade too late. With today's communications climate, it's not hard to understand how vitally important it is to start taking action now. Therefore we have not attempted such a wildly ambitious task. Instead, our methodology was qualitative. We heavily relied on our experienced interviewees.

Throughout the book, we occasionally refer to the five 'players' in agricultural communication: consumers, farmers, agribusiness, policymakers, and academics. We periodically use these players as a lens through which to view certain elements or perspectives. In addition, we also use the term 'production agriculture' – or what may also be known as 'intensive agriculture' – to denote a large-scale system with a focus on achieving the highest output possible with the lowest input or the lowest cost. When using the overarching term 'agriculture,' we reference a broad umbrella group of people who are part of the agricultural community. This is more than farmers and farm workers, but also the associations or other groups that represent farmers. Furthermore, it includes the agribusinesses that sell inputs or equipment to farmers, or those that are involved in the distribution and sale of farm commodities. We clarify when we are referring to just farmers, or just agribusinesses.

The book is separated into three clear parts. Part I highlights relevant, recent examples of unreliable or confusing communication that has had a large and lasting impact on consumer opinions or has had real economic impact. We purposefully selected our examples to cover a broad range of issues, covering matters such as 'pink slime,' Chipotle's marketing techniques, celebrity bloggers, and more. Our examples aren't meant to cast judgment, but to demonstrate where no communication or extreme and careless messaging misleads well-intentioned consumers.

Part II digs into the *why* and *how*. This section humanizes the players in agriculture and shares some of the underlying elements that influence how we communicate in this field. It lays the groundwork so we, consumers and agricultural professionals, can begin to ponder how information is shared between us and how it might be improved.

The final part, Part III, concerns our future. We reflect on how we can seek 'common ground' to facilitate difficult communication.

Common ground is not an idealistic, vague concept, but a real solution for enhancing dialogue and communication. This does not imply that disagreements aren't productive; on the contrary, they are often the healthiest discussions we can have. However, we need to allow for this type of environment, one where we can hear a more diverse and reasoned set of opinions. In this way, we can create a space for previously unimaginable, creative innovation to unfold.

To conclude, each one of us needs to take personal ownership of better communication around food and agriculture. Our current incentive systems don't always drive us to include all groups or opinions, so we need to think more creatively about how all voices can be heard. As we will see in the following pages, shying away from conversations is only exacerbating the damage, delaying real conversations, and deepening the divide.

PART I
The reality

From the ick factor of 'pink slime,' a company's ruthlessly efficient marketing campaign to the allure of celebrities' unscientific health advice and more, Part I tackles a carefully selected sample of challenges that underscore the reality of modern communication. Broken down into five chapters, it presents a stark, no-nonsense picture of today's agricultural conversation in its entirety.

1

PINK SLIME

When a media frenzy strikes

American consumers love beef. Ground beef is a particular favorite for home-cooked meals, eaten with gusto in kitchens across the nation. Some 60 percent of beef consumption in kitchens around America is ground beef.[1] To get into the nitty gritty, which these families generally don't, ground beef is produced from any part of the boneless beef carcass. It must have no more than 30 percent fat and contain no added water, phosphates, binders, or extenders.[2]

There is a company in South Dakota, named Beef Products, Inc. (BPI), which manufactures boneless lean beef. They were established in 1981 and as demand for beef products grew, so did they. In 1991, the company decided to minimize waste in the meat industry. They started to take the lean trimmings from other processing facilities and create a byproduct. These trimmings were mostly fat and a little strip of protein. In processing trimmings that would normally have gone to waste, they were able to extract the sliver of red meat that was usually tossed out with the fat. From this, they produced a product known within the industry as lean finely textured beef (LFTB).[3]

In 2011, British celebrity chef Jamie Oliver decided to tackle the issue of LFTB in his popular TV show *Jamie Oliver's Food Revolution*.[4]

He began the segment by bringing a live cow, named Scarlett, in front of a smiling audience of wholesome children and parents. Scarlett wanders calmly to the center of the set and stands peacefully, oblivious to the absurdity of her situation. The camera pans to a smiling young mother with a child in her arms.

"We're going to show you a little story about beef!" quips Oliver in his cheery British accent. He walks around the live cow and shows them where the different cuts are and how much each one costs on the market. Scarlett's body has been portioned off, presumably by chalk, to demonstrate her various consumable parts. Educational, one might think.

"Why am I doing all this? Did you come down here for a meat lesson?" Apparently not. Jamie Oliver, in a made-for-TV moment of drama, makes it clear that he is not doing this to teach us about the various cuts of the cow. He's here to teach us about the horrors of trimmings. The scene theatrically flashes to Oliver sitting against a black backdrop, leaning forward. "In my industry, we call those trimmings sh★★. Get rid of them."

Camera cut back to the studio, Oliver takes some cow trimmings and walks boldly out into the crowd of parents and kids. He aggressively shoves the meat into the audience's faces. They pull back in disgust (which begs the question, who wouldn't pull back in disgust if an aggressive man in a plaid shirt shoved raw meat in your face?). But the message has been sent.

"So first thing, this is how I imagined the process to be ... they take all those trimmings ... they put it in a centrifuge and they spin it. And what does that do? It splits the fat from the meat and separates it," says Oliver. He takes his bucket of trimmings and puts it in a dryer. Once it has run for a few moments, he removes the separated meat. He returns to his audience of families and children and shoves this new bucket of meat into their faces. Cue cringing and disgust. A petite, blond-haired little girl stares in horror. The camera zooms in on her innocent face.

Oliver dumps the bits of meat in a bin and opens a child-locked drawer full of household cleaning elements, oh-so-carefully placed at camera level so as to highlight his dramatic unlocking of the drawer. He takes out a larger container of ammonia (clearly marked ammonia in large print, visible to the camera) and dumps it on the meat. He mixes it up with his hands and then dumps it through a grinder. Lo and behold, Jamie Oliver created 'pink slime' as he, direct quote, "imagined the process to be."

Imagination and Jamie Oliver aside, the reality of LFTB is somewhat more nuanced. A substantial portion of a beef carcass, about 25 percent, is lean beef trimmings.[5] BPI was taking what would otherwise be wasted food and finding a purpose for it. This lean textured beef was considered ideal to sell to school lunch programs, fast food chains like McDonald's, and other people making hamburgers. If you added it into hamburger beef, it could increase the leanness and create the perfect lean-to-fat ratio.

Amongst other processes to ensure food safety, Beef Products Inc. used a common intervention in the industry – they blasted the product with a small amount of ammonia. Ammonia in food is not new, nor is it rare.[6] There is a natural amount of pure ammonium hydroxide in beef already. BPI increased this by a minute amount because it is a powerful defense against potential germs. It was thoroughly reviewed and approved by the United States Department of Agriculture (USDA) and the Food and Drug Administration (FDA), as ammonia has proven to be one of the most effective advances in food safety today. It's used in several other areas of the industry, including processing of baked goods, cheeses, and chocolate. With LFTB, USDA deemed it to be a processing aid and not an ingredient in the beef so they didn't require it to be posted on the label.[7]

It wasn't Oliver who coined the term 'pink slime,' a name subsequently picked up and touted by US media that came to haunt BPI. A 2009 article in the *New York Times* noted opposition to LFTB by two former USDA employees, dating back to the USDA's approval of ammonium hydroxide more than ten years prior. An internal email that became public as part of a *New York Times* Freedom of Information Act request contained the term 'pink slime.'[8]

The well-researched 2009 *New York Times* article brought little national attention to the issue. Jamie Oliver's show dramatized the matter and started building momentum. Soon after, in 2012, *ABC* decided to pick up the story.[9] It was then that public backlash to LFTB launched in earnest.[10] *ABC* produced a series of reports and the matter snowballed. Other media picked up the story and it stormed the nation. In a rapid turn of events, food activists and consumers around the country were suddenly and actively involved in a "Stop Pink Slime" movement.

What happened? LFTB, and subsequently BPI, fell victim to a voracious media frenzy. The results were dire. As *Reuters* reported in March of 2013, the company was devastated: "Today, the South Dakota company's revenues have plummeted from more than $650 million to about $130 million a year, and three of its plants are shuttered. Company officials blame the abrupt falloff on a series of ABC News broadcasts that began last March – stories that repeatedly called its product 'pink slime.'"[11] BPI reported that more than 700 employees lost their jobs as a result of the furor.[12]

Chris Waldrop's job as the Director of the Food Policy Institute at Consumer Federation of America is to promote food safety measures across government and industry to protect consumers. He is literally paid to make sure that consumer interest is represented on food safety decisions. In an interview with us, he explained the 'pink slime' issue and how it got so wildly out of control: "It is said that they [*ABC*] were sort of blurring the line between safety and the 'ick factor.' A lot of people thought that it was icky and didn't want to eat it and they didn't want their kids to be eating it. There was a lot of confusion between is it safe or is it just gross." Consumers generally don't fully understand where their food comes from, so when they hear about it for the first time, their immediate response may be, "I don't want to eat that!"[13] Waldrop, a consumer advocate, was not concerned about the safety of LFTB. In fact, with tempered frustration, he expressed his wish to mobilize consumers on other issues that warranted far more real concern.

The 24-hour media cycle got their fingers into something and they needed to fill airtime and get their ratings up. Consumers, concerned about their food, got swept along in a tide of righteous anger. As Waldrop said, "The nature of the media cycle is that you have reporters that just need to get something out quick, and so they may not spend as much time on it as they need to or probably should." As such, consumers did not get the whole story, but neither were they actively looking for it. There's nothing quite as catchy as 'pink slime' to get people paying attention, and people like gross, we pay attention to gross.

The repercussions of this massive miscommunication were real and severe – lost revenue, damaged reputations, increased waste, and more than 700 employees lost their jobs. As outrage has subsided and with beef prices hovering around an all-time high while school lunch budgets are tight, schools are once again embracing LFTB. Never having been conclusively proven to damage health, this low-cost and waste-saving product is creeping back onto the shelves.

Consumer influence is growing in a changing media landscape where information flows easily and quickly and is not always fact-checked. This increased influence has real consequences in the agricultural industry. "The LFTB controversy demonstrates that consumers' perceptions and understanding of modern food production can quickly affect markets and/or a company's business," reported Joel L. Green, an analyst in agricultural policy for the Congressional Research Service.[14]

There is no turning back the clock. We live in a new age of information. J. Ross Pruitt and Joshua D. Detre, when both professors at Louisiana State University Agricultural Center, wrote that a lack of transparency at various levels of the agricultural supply chain contributed to the public backlash against the inclusion of LFTB in a variety of outlets. They concluded, "Educating consumers about food production is a challenge not to be ignored."[15] We are no longer in a time where public relations crises will blow over in a couple days if kicked under the rug. On the contrary, ignoring a crisis will make the public suspect that there is something to hide.

Would better transparency have stood up to a major news network's characterization of LFTB as 'pink slime'? Perhaps, but perhaps not entirely. However, it would most certainly have diminished the intensity of the media frenzy or even prevented it from reaching such a heightened point in the first place. Enhanced transparency means communicating to consumers and stakeholders about what is going on 'behind the scenes' – in other words, anticipating what people should or would like to know and providing the information to them in a controlled manner. As demonstrated in this case, doing so – or neglecting to do so – can carry significant economic weight in today's world.

Notes

1 National Cattlemen's Beef Association, "Beef Industry Statistics," Average Annual Per Capita Consumption, Beef Cuts and Ground Beef, and Beef at a Glance, January 2012, http://www.beefusa.org/beefindustrystatistics.aspx.
2 9 C.F.R. §319.15 (a). According to the regulation, ground beef may also contain beef cheek meat, but if it exceeds 25% by volume, it must be noted on the label. Extenders are described by the National Meat Association (NMA) as cereals, legumes, vegetables, roots, and tubers. Available at https://www.gpo.gov/fdsys/granule/CFR-2012-title9-vol2/CFR-2012-title9-vol2-sec319-15.
3 Information on BPI is available at http://www.beefproducts.com/index.php.
4 "Jamie Oliver's Food Revolution: Pink Slime—70% of America's Beef Is Treated with Ammonia," https://www.youtube.com/watch?v=J1Z6AgHthJs. Accessed on June 23, 2015.
5 John R. Romans et al. (1994) *The Meat We Eat*, Danville, IL: Interstate Publishers, Inc., p. 591.
6 International Food Information Council Foundation, Food Insight, "Questions and Answers about Ammonium Hydroxide Use in Food Production," December 29, 2009. See http://www.foodinsight.org/Resources/Detail.aspx?topic=Questions_and_Answers_about_Ammonium_Hydroxide_Use_in_Food_Production.
7 USDA, Food Safety and Inspection Service, Compliance Guide on the Determination of Processing Aids, April 8, 2008, http://www.fsis.usda.gov/pdf/determination_of_processing_aids.pdf.
8 Michael Moss (2009) "Safety of Beef Processing Method Is Questioned," *New York Times*, December 31, http://www.nytimes.com/2009/12/31/us/31meat.html?pagewanted=all.
9 Jim Avila, "70 Percent of Ground Beef at Supermarkets Contains 'Pink Slime'," *ABC News*, March 7, 2012. Video available at http://abcnews.go.com/blogs/headlines/2012/03/70-percent-of-ground-beef-at-supermarkets-contains-pink-slime/.
10 J. Pruitt and D. Anderson (2012) "Assessing the Impact of LFTB in the Beef Cattle Industry." Retrieved November 28, 2015, from http://www.choicesmagazine.org/choices-magazine/theme-articles/pink-slimemarketing-uncertainty-and-risk-in-the-24-hour-news-cycle/assessing-the-impact-of-lftb-in-the-beef-cattle-industry.

11 P. J. Huffstutter and Martha Graybow, "SPECIAL REPORT—Did Diane Sawyer Smear 'Pink Slime'?," Reuters, March 4, 2013, http://www.reuters.com/article/2013/03/04/usa-media-abc-bpi-id USL1N0B42VT20130304.

12 BPI Press Release, "BPI Files Suit against ABC for Disinformation Campaign," September 13, 2012, http://www.beefproducts.com/press_releases.php.

13 Chris Waldrop, telephone interview, June 2015.

14 Joel L. Green, "Lean Finely Textured Beef: The 'Pink Slime' Controversy," Congressional Research Service, April 6, 2012, http://www.nationalaglawcenter.org/wp-content/uploads/assets/crs/R42473.pdf.

15 J. Pruitt and J. Detre (2012) "Theme Overview: Pink Slime, Marketing, Uncertainty, and Risk in the 24 Hour News Cycle." Retrieved November 28, 2015, from http://www.choicesmagazine.org/choices-magazine/theme-articles/pink-slimemarketing-uncertainty-and-risk-in-the-24-hour-news-cycle/theme-overview-pink-slime-marketing-uncertainty-and-risk-in-the-24-hour-news-cycle.

2

CHIPOTLE MARKETING

Pushing polarization to the next level

There are certain restaurant chains now and certain groups advertising non-GMO in their product ... By the very manner of approaching this, the public is being given the impression that something potentially dangerous is occurring in their food supply.

(Former United States Senator Richard G. Lugar,
President of The Lugar Center)

Most people think of Chipotle Mexican Grill™ as the company that changed the way fast food is delivered. The atmosphere and experience in a Chipotle restaurant are quite different from many other fast food chains. The kitchen is exposed for immediate inspection and food is fresh, wholesome, simple. The industrial decor makes the place feel clean and progressive. The employees are held to high standards; they're fast and efficient.

However, it was much more than an atmospheric makeover and delivery of a freshly cooked product that made Chipotle so wildly successful. It was their marketing. They responded to consumer interest in health and food in a powerful and extremely effective way. To do this, they successfully distinguished themselves by turning to a new form of marketing, one that is largely focused on public relations. With commendable creativity, Chipotle created a fairytale world of good and evil, a world ideal for soundbites and short attention spans. This world plays off of consumer confusion over complex food issues, and positions Chipotle as the 'good guy' trying to save consumers.

From the colorful and conspicuous billboards lining the sides of our highways to the television in our dentist's office touting the newest toothpaste, advertising is everywhere. What and how businesses communicate with their consumers is a massive part of our economy. In our new age of web interactions and social media, the consumer has the power and platform to discuss and share openly with an instantly available, like-minded friend network. Companies have had to find new and creative approaches to wooing and then maintaining loyal customers.

Despite damages to sales and reputation from a series of food-related illnesses in 2015,[1] Chipotle has experienced immense success. They were ranked on *Forbes*'s 2015 The World's Most Innovative Companies and were listed as having a market cap of $20.5 billion in May 2015.[2] They were featured in *Fast Company* as one of The World's Top 10 Most Innovative Companies in Food.[3] The *Wall Street Journal* published an article entitled, "The Chipotle Effect: How Chefs Are Reinventing Fast Food."[4] The list goes on. But what does this have to do with agriculture?

Chipotle's success is twofold – they reinvented fast food, but they also leveraged a unique form of communication with consumers, and this communication is centered around the denigration of many elements of modern agriculture and, by association, the fast food competition. Chipotle used a unique blend of public relations and corporate social responsibility to market themselves. Part of their public relations strategy is portraying parts of agriculture as the 'bad guy.'

Companies now, more than ever, are trying to show how they care by adopting some form of corporate social responsibility.[5] Consumers are beginning to think beyond how a product makes them look and feel or how it hits their pocketbook. They're thinking about the environmental and social implications of that product and that interest is sincere. Some consumers are even willing to pay more for products that have characteristics that are environmentally and socially conscious. Chipotle's marketing model has met these ideals and values by framing some issues in a way that appear educational but on closer inspection fall far short of presenting a balanced perspective.

Chipotle has built a brand personality that is centered on sincerity. They don't use traditional marketing. Rather, they engage with the community and connect with consumers on a deep emotional level through their corporate social responsibility campaigns. 'Food with Integrity' is the slogan Chipotle management chose in their quest to frame their brand personality. The intention is to communicate to their audience that they are doing something more meaningful than just feeding you wholesome, simple food. They want to relay a responsibility to consumers, the environment, and to animals.

A case study in the *International Journal of Strategic Communication* looks at how Chipotle purposefully communicates their corporate social responsibility programs to their public. "Chipotle views the public relations, branding and marketing efforts of the organization as *synergized* rather than *competing* organization forces," write the authors. Chipotle has integrated these multiple functions into a cohesive strategy to build customer trust and loyalty. "Chipotle's most devoted public, the members of its brand community, indeed perceive sincerity to be the most salient dimension of Chipotle's brand personality," the case study concludes.[6] They are credited by others as having obtained such great marketing success by using nontraditional tactics such as word of mouth techniques[7] and a keen responsiveness to values, in particular millennial values.[8]

The tactics Chipotle has employed have been incredibly effective. They share common threads: easy to understand, entertaining, emotional, and of course sincere. The trust they build with their audience serves to magnify the power of their communication of brand and product. Some of these tactics are community events and sponsorship as well as the use of videos and ultimately their website.

Community events and sponsorships have enabled Chipotle to reach consumers on a more personal level and this approach has served them well. Local marketing personnel get involved in schools and local organizations to share the 'Food with Integrity' message.[9]

They hold Free Burrito giveaway days. Another example is Chipotle's Cultivate Festival, a festival of 'food, music and ideas' that was held in Phoenix, Kansas City, and Minneapolis in 2015 alone. The event boasts concerts, Chef Demos, and educational exhibits. A GMO exhibit boasts visually appealing infographics with large letters that state, "GMOs have not yet been proven safe to eat" and "The use of GMOs can damage the environment." People can choose which GMO issue "concerns you the most" and they get to put a yellow ping pong ball into a little vacuum tube. On the other side, you can see the issues 'filling up.' The event exudes trustworthiness, concern, and wholesomeness. Everything is presented in a clear, simple, and very brief manner, as if to say, 'See? These issues aren't confusing.'

A second extremely powerful communication tactic is their aesthetic, heartfelt commercials, YouTube videos, and entertaining mini-series. Their "Back to the Start" YouTube video has had nearly ten million views. Coldplay's classic "The Scientist" is performed in the background by country music legend Willie Nelson. There are no words, just animation. With cute blow-up characters, it is intended to capture the evolution of the hog industry – from a lone pig alongside an adorable farming family (replete with babe in arms) to an assembly line of hogs behind jail cell bars that are put on a conveyer belt and pumped with pills and processed. A cartoon character finally becomes frustrated with this newly evolved 'pig system' and the inspirational music builds until the farmer decides to get away from it all and go back to the start. Land flips over and is instantaneously converted to beautiful countryside so the pigs are raised outside on green pastures where life is good again. The weather is perfect. It ends with the farmer, happy again, loading up a crate into a Chipotle truck while his family watches on.[10]

"The Scarecrow" video has over 15 million views on YouTube. It is a companion film for Chipotle's app-based game. The scarecrow is an everyday worker who punches into a giant food processing factory that looks like something out of a science fiction movie. Mechanized crows with burning red eyes watch over the factory workers as they fill boxes stamped with the label "100% beef-ish!" The scarecrow sees chickens being injected by machine people and instantly doubling in size. He sees cows completely enclosed in metal boxes with only their heads peeking out as they are being horrifically milked. Exasperated by what he has witnessed, the scarecrow goes home and picks fresh vegetables from his garden, loads them up on a truck and starts a makeshift burrito stand of his own.[11]

Taking this even further, they produced an original series called *Farmed and Dangerous*. This four-episode series of approximately 20-minute segments is described on their website as a "Chipotle original comedy series that explores the outrageously twisted and utterly unsustainable world of industrial agriculture." It is a satire of modern agriculture, featuring a fictional megacorporation, Animoil, that feeds cows 'petropellets' made directly from petroleum. To get a sense for the style, a cow explodes after eating 'petropellets.' A man records and releases a video about it and then Animoil targets him for leaking the truth.[12]

These videos, ranging from commercials to animated YouTube stories and even to original mini-dramas, do not portray reality. The American Society of Animal Sciences released a statement from their Board of Directors: "Chipotle sells twisted image of animal agriculture," in response to a commercial aired during the Grammy Awards. Their take-away: Chipotle misrepresents. In their statement, they highlighted that banning antimicrobial use in animal production is likely to create a welfare issue, outdoor housing systems for pigs create new animal welfare problems such as biting and injuring each other to assert dominance, and Chipotle rarely used USDA-certified organic products (preferring instead to purchase pork from producers who follow their own "naturally raised" guidelines). The statement concludes: "Chipotle, like any company, is advertising a fantasy. Coca-Cola has smiling polar bears, Old Spice has manly men and Chipotle has a cartoon farm. Chipotle did not try to represent science or agriculture truthfully; instead, it made a commercial."[13]

Their website is an important communications tool in their campaign. Chipotle does what they do best on this site: make the tough issues seem easy. Their "Food with Integrity" take on GMOs, introduced on their site as 'G-M-Over it,' is presented in a way that is very simple to navigate. They use extra-large bold font for their main message. When a user clicks on it, they get even larger font enticing them to drill a little further, dig a little bit more. Click again and they get a mix of medium and small font.[14] The experience of clicking around the website in itself gives you a sense of "digging into the issue," researching it for yourself, and learning more and more as you go. The verbiage is carefully worded so the GMO issue appears balanced and fully considered. Just as Apple has done with personal computing, Chipotle breaks down complex issues to something that seems so simple and refined ('seems' – not 'is').

"There are many companies who are spending a great deal of money attempting to influence public opinion on GMOs," said Former United States Senator Richard G. Lugar, President of The Lugar Center and Chairman of the Senate Committee on Agriculture, Nutrition, and Forestry, in an interview with us. "The Chipotle restaurants have decided to use the anti-GMO element as a way of boosting their company by saying, 'If you come here, you're not going to have GMOs. You're not going to be hit by this bad stuff that's coming along.' So in other words, we have firms actually advertising in that way to promote their own particular brand competitively – which I think is very mistaken."

Chipotle could appeal to consumers with facts, not by making a comedy sketch of agriculture. They could promote the strategy of their business model without belittling other models. They could educate without invoking unnecessary fears. The reality, however, is that Chipotle is not an educational institution. It is well within their rights to market to consumers as they please using whatever strategy they find most effective. Chipotle is doing what every company's marketing department does every single day, in every move they make – responding to consumer demand and interest, and seeking to increase market share.

USA Today quoted Nicole Patterson, a corn and hog farmer in Decatur County, Iowa, who said, "For them it's a smart marketing ploy, but for us farmers it's unfortunate because they are using fear and twisting the truth. I would challenge Chipotle … to get out to the farms they are putting down, to the family farms like mine that they are calling factory farms."[15]

Chipotle has established an image that is smart, progressive, wholesome, and sincere. Never mind that they are a corporation, they may be the ones people are listening to when it comes to matters such as GMOs and agriculture. Senator Lugar explained, "Right now, it's a battle of public opinion. It's a question of whether those of us in agriculture and those who have been doing scientific studies are able to make our case strongly enough and influence public opinion sufficiently that we overcome the fears and the phobias that are being created."

Marketing is a powerful form of communication. Chipotle has developed a unique way to brand themselves and communicate with consumers about agriculture. They are doing so effectively, but in the process they denigrate agriculture to boost their corporate success. Consumer confusion over agricultural issues is rampant. Chipotle plays into this by building fear; they are then uniquely positioned to prove to customers that they care. Chipotle communicates a stark black and white world. They project a world in which agriculture is simple and easy to understand, but this image misleads consumers about what agriculture really is.

Chipotle experienced a setback at the end of 2015 after outbreaks of E. coli triggered concern over the company's ability to live up to a promise central to their success – delivering customers fresh and local food. Media outlets called into question Chipotle's heavily promoted 'Food with Integrity' slogan. There were two separate outbreaks, one that infected 55 people in 11 states, and another that infected 5 people in 3 states.[16] The Centers for Disease Control and Prevention (CDC) conducted an investigation of the cases.

Chipotle's stock indicates the extent of the damage. The price went from $745 in October 2015 to $404 in January 2016. After the CDC closed the investigation the stock price began to bounce back; however, it remains to be seen what the long-term damage will be to the company and how it will change perceptions in their loyal fan base. In the past, food related illnesses have resulted in long-term damage, with some of the more extreme cases resulting in hefty lawsuit payouts.[17] This type of negative coverage is not quickly forgotten and prior incidences resurface when news of new outbreaks in other restaurants occur. How the company chooses to implement new supply chain policies and how successful these are at avoiding future outbreaks will play a role in determining the outcome.

Notes

1 R. Abrams (2016) "Chipotle Is Subpoenaed in Criminal Inquiry Over Norovirus Outbreak." Retrieved January 29, 2016, from http://www. nytimes.com/2016/01/07/business/chipotle-outbreak.html?_r=0.
2 "#24 Chipotle Mexican Grill." *Forbes*. Forbes Magazine. 1 May 2015. Web. 1 October 2015. http://www.forbes.com/companies/chipotle-mexican-grill/.
3 "The World's Top 10 Most Innovative Companies in Food." *Fast Company*. 31 March 2014. Web. 1 October 2015. http://www.fastcompany.com/3026682/most-innovative-companies-2014/the-worlds-top-10-most-innovative-companies-in-food.
4 Jay Cheshes, "The Chipotle Effect: How Chefs Are Reinventing Fast Food." *Wall Street Journal*. 6 February 2015. Web. 1 October 2015.
5 Karen L. Becker-Olsen, B. Andrew Cudmore, and Ronald Paul Hill (2006) "The Impact of Perceived Corporate Social Responsibility on Consumer Behavior," *Journal of Business Research* 59(1): 46–53.
6 M. Ragas and M. Roberts (2009) "Communicating Corporate Social Responsibility and Brand Sincerity: A Case Study of Chipotle Mexican Grill's 'Food with Integrity' Program," *International Journal of Strategic Communication*, 3(4): 264–280.
7 "9 Examples of How Chipotle's Word-of-Mouth Marketing Strategy Works Its Magic – Word-of-Mouth and Referral Marketing Blog" (2015, July 1) Retrieved November 15, 2015, from http://www.referralcandy.com/blog/9-examples-of-how-chipotles-word-of-mouth-marketing-strategy-works-its-magic/.
8 S. Davis (2014, June 6) "Beyond the Burrito: Chipotle's Next Big Move." Retrieved November 15, 2015, from http://www.forbes.com/sites/scottdavis/2014/06/06/beyond-the-burrito-chipotles-next-big-move/.
9 M. Ragas and M. Roberts (2009) "Communicating Corporate Social Responsibility and Brand Sincerity: A Case Study of Chipotle Mexican Grill's 'Food with Integrity' Program," *International Journal of Strategic Communication*, 3(4): 264–280.
10 "Back to the Start" (n.d.) Retrieved November 15, 2015, from https://www.youtube.com/watch?v=aMfSGt6rHos.
11 "The Scarecrow" (n.d.) Retrieved November 15, 2015, from https://www.youtube.com/watch?v=lUtnas5ScSE.
12 *Farmed and Dangerous*, Chipotle Original Series (n.d.) Retrieved October 16, 2015, from http://farmedanddangerous.com/.
13 "Chipotle Sells Twisted Image of Animal Agriculture" (n.d.) Retrieved October 16, 2015, from https://www.asas.org/membership-services/

press-room/board-statement-archive/chipotle-sells-twisted-image-of-animal-agriculture.
14 "G-M-Over It" (n.d.) Retrieved November 15, 2015, from http://chipotle.com/GMO.
15 C. Bureau (2014, March 3) "Chipotle's Farm Satire Upsets Agriculture Industry." Retrieved October 17, 2015, from http://www.usatoday.com/story/news/politics/2014/03/03/chipotle-show-angers-farmers/5874435/.
16 "Multistate Outbreaks of Shiga Toxin-producing Escherichia coli O26 Infections Linked to Chipotle Mexican Grill Restaurants (Final Update)" (2016) Retrieved February 2, 2016, from http://www.cdc.gov/ecoli/2015/o26-11-15/.
17 "10 Notable E. coli Outbreaks at U.S. Fast-food Restaurants" (n.d.) Retrieved February 2, 2016, from http://www.upi.com/Health_News/2015/12/31/10-notable-E-coli-outbreaks-at-US-fast-food-restaurants/5781451489618/.

3

ALL THAT GLITTERS

The power of non-expert influence

On April 21, 2015, the *Washington Post* ran an article titled "Kraft Mac & Cheese just got duller. You can thank (or blame) 'The Food Babe.'" As far as headlines go, this one is exceptional in capturing the wide range of emotions their varied readership would experience at the news. Not an easy task for a headline.

As journalist Michael E. Miller writes so eloquently in this article, "Nothing triggers nostalgia like the sight of a steaming plate of sticky pasta, as unnaturally orange as a nuclear dawn."[1] Yet the color of our fondest childhood memories will soon be gone, Miller tells us. Kraft Mac & Cheese just announced that it is stripping all artificial preservatives and synthetic colors from its most iconic item.

We are to attribute this change to 'The Food Babe.' You may be familiar with this woman, or you may be asking yourself, "What?" "Who?" "She's a woman, then?" (Or, in my case, wondering if I could ever find the sheer verve to start calling myself 'The Writing Babe.' The answer to that would be a resounding no.)

The Food Babe's real name is Vani Hari. She has nearly a million followers on Twitter, over a million 'likes' on Facebook and claims three million unique readers on her blog.[2] She is a blogging and social media queen. A former computer science major with no academic training as a food scientist, nutritionist or chef, she has managed to become a major voice in our national conversations on food. She has targeted Starbucks (accusations of "hazardous chemicals" in pumpkin spice lattes), Chick-fil-A (which she called Chemical-Fil-A), Whole Foods (for genetically modified and hidden ingredients), and Subway. To protest the sandwich chain's use of azodicarbonamide in its bread, Ms. Hari posted a video of herself chewing another item in which the chemical is found: a yoga mat.[3]

Hari's story of redemption is undeniably intriguing, although certainly not new. She was once overweight and unhealthy – she didn't think about what she ate and didn't take care of her diet. Now, after making a revolutionary change in her approach to food, she has transformed into a slim, beautiful spokesperson for health with long shiny hair and flawless photographs. She even has a 'before' and 'after' photo highlighting her impressive transition on her blog. Her mission is to guide others to success and health with her self-taught nutrition.[4]

In the battle against Kraft's use of dyes in Mac & Cheese, Hari teamed up with another blogging phenomenon, Lisa Leake of 100DaysofRealFood.com. Leake is a mom and her claim to fame is her battle to feed her family 'real food.' Pictures of Lisa's smiling face, alongside her husband and two daughters, adorn her website.[5] She has a quarter million followers on Twitter and 1.5 million likes on Facebook. Leake and Hari mean business (and are, of course, in business). Both Hari and Leake have books for sale. Unfortunately, neither of the two responded to requests for interviews.

Hari and Leake launched a petition against Kraft because of dyes Yellow No. 5 and Yellow No. 6 in their signature Macaroni & Cheese. Their major argument is that we, in America, deserve the same treatment as our British counterparts. In the United Kingdom, Kraft does not put the same dyes in their Mac & Cheese. In a 2½-minute video call-to-action online, these two camera-friendly and relatable women stare up at the lens with earnest eyes and plead to the American public that they make their voices heard and demand the same treatment as their UK counterparts.

They carefully highlight the two versions of Mac & Cheese – American style and UK style. (UK calls it "Cheesey Pasta." Who knew?) They've even gone to the trouble of preparing both the UK's Cheesey Pasta and America's Mac & Cheese in the video. On camera, they actually take nibbles off the two different plates to prove that there's no taste difference. Admittedly a rather hard point to prove, particularly when Leake can barely hide her disgust while spearing two tiny noodles from the US version of Mac & Cheese.

"Artificial food dyes have been proven to increase hyperactivity in children, negatively affect their ability to learn and they also cause other health problems such as asthma, skin rashes and migraines as well," states Leake in the video. These claims are reiterated in the text on the website immediately below the video, with no hyperlinks to any studies or research.[6]

Their campaign was a success, a brilliant one in fact. As Miller writes, "This isn't the first time that Hari has scored an unlikely victory over a food giant. Over the past year, she has emerged as a powerful – if not always reliable – voice in the debate over nutrition." He continues, "Hari hasn't helped her cause by getting some things spectacularly wrong. In a post that she later removed from her Website, she said that microwaves destroy the nutritional content of food and 'create severe health issues.' In another, also deleted, post, she argued that flying causes a traveler's 'digestive organs [to] start to shrink, taxing your ability to digest large quantities of food. Secondly, this compression reduces the ability for your body to normally circulate blood through your blood vessels.'"

Hari's campaign tactics are clear-cut. She masterfully uses fear, worry, and disgust to mobilize her fan base and attract more visitors to her blog. Hari and Leake are passionate, relatable, and have positioned themselves well to be heard and be influential over a growing niche of the population with whom their message resonates. Some of their victories are innocuous (although Kraft may not agree), such as removing dyes from our Mac & Cheese. Yet others aren't so innocent. Scientists are starting to lash out at Hari, particularly chemists, most notably in an article in *Gawker* by analytical chemist Yvette d'Entremont, "The 'Food Babe' Blogger Is Full of Shit."

D'Entremont has, evidently, decided to fight fire with fire. If Hari was going to use inflammatory language, well so was she.

Hari's superhero origin story is that she came down with appendicitis and didn't accept the explanation that appendicitis just happens sometimes. So she quit her job as a consultant, attended Google University and transformed herself into an uncredentialed expert in everything she admittedly can't pronounce. Slap the catchy moniker "Food Babe" on top, throw in a couple of trend stories and some appearances on the Dr. Oz show, and we have the new organic media darling.[7]

D'Entremont pretty much nails it in her fiery article. She outlines one by one Hari's worst offenses. She is spreading fear of anything that isn't 'natural,' organic, or GMO-free. She condemns those who disagree with her as having ties to sinister organizations. She has crusaded against 610 products and companies to date. Hari thinks it's okay to lie about your food allergies. In d'Entremont's article, the list goes on, detailed meticulously with examples and hyperlinks that back up her statements.

Vani Hari is one of many, many bloggers who have taken the internet by storm and changed the way we interact and interplay with information. Companies, looking to their bottom line, quickly learned that a great tactic to boost sales was to pay leading bloggers in their industry to write up their products positively. Many a blogger either lives by, or supplements their lifestyle off, the proceeds of advertising dollars dependent on the volume of traffic their site can capture. Some bloggers are responsible, some aren't. There are no gatekeepers, whatsoever, to the type of information that can be put on a blog. We are a country that prizes freedom of speech – even when it is inaccurate.

Vani Hari and Lisa Leake, just two women, were able to get a huge conglomerate to make a change to their signature product. What sort of power do they wield that they were able to get 365,000 Americans to sign an online petition over pasta? How did #FoodBabeArmy really become a *thing*?

What Hari, and other food bloggers, are playing off of – either intentionally or unintentionally – is consumer confusion about their food. Technology in agriculture is changing rapidly and the general public is being confronted with concepts and ideas they have never heard of before. Are GMOs safe? Should I only eat organic? Are chemicals used in the food system hurting my family and me? Should I only buy local? What about animal welfare?

These matters are *confusing*. To truly understand them is time consuming. There are no classes that teach citizens the basics of food production. Reliable information is nearly impossible to find. In today's food and agriculture information climate, it takes an expert and a lot of time to sift through the junk that's out there to find balanced and informative sources – and for that information to actually be consumable and understandable? Even harder still.

Trying to measure the power and influence of food bloggers is slippery. The most relevant scholarly article on the matter concluded with the "need for further research using the food-blogging communities."[8] There has not been an outpouring of such research in the five years since that resounding conclusion was put forth.

BlogHer, a media company of online influencers, launched a study about the influence of food blogs on food-related decisions. They sampled 1,766 women and 323 men. The methodology was not released, but they claim that 71 percent of 18–44 year olds have made a food purchase based on a blog recommendation.[9] These findings are to be taken with a grain of salt (they are, after all, a blog that promotes blogging and they did a study demonstrating the influence of food blogs).

Hari's pseudo-science claims and attacks on scientists trigger angry responses from the science community, some of whom take shots right back at her. Understandable, in that she can be dismissive and indeed downright derogatory towards academics and scientists who have devoted their lives to discovering and exploring truths for the general welfare of society. Not to mention that scientists feel like they have to be angry right back to get any kind of traction with the population – or coverage by the media, for that matter.

More than offending chemists around the world, Hari and many other bloggers are not looking to find common ground – they are looking to spark outrage. Why? Outrage is so very attractive and contagious in its simplicity, and 'so very contagious' is a part of their business model. The unique views for any blog will skyrocket. And, as we have seen in the case of Kraft, companies will make changes.

Are they the changes we actually need? In some cases, unfortunately not. Therein lies the crux of the matter.

Notes

1 Michael Miller, "Kraft Mac & Cheese Just Got Duller. You Can Thank (or Blame) 'The Food Babe'." *Washington Post*, 21 April 2015, Morning Mix sec. Web. http://www.washingtonpost.com/news/morning-mix/wp/2015/04/21/kraft-mac-cheese-just-got-duller-you-can-thank-or-blame-the-food-babe/.

2 Dan Schawbel, "Vani Hari: How She Grew Her Food Blog into an Empire." *Forbes*. Forbes Magazine. Web. 4 September 2015. http://www.forbes.com/sites/danschawbel/2015/02/10/vani-hari-how-she-grew-her-food-blog-into-an-empire/.

3 C. Rubin (2015, March 13) "Taking On the Food Industry, One Blog Post at a Time." Retrieved September 19, 2015. http://www.nytimes.com/2015/03/15/style/taking-on-the-food-industry-one-blog-post-at-a-time.html.

4 "About Vani Hari the 'Food Babe' – Join Me and Investigate Your Food." *Food Babe*. Web. 4 September 2015. http://foodbabe.com/about-me/.

5 "100 Days of Real Food." *100 Days of Real Food*. Web. 4 September 2015. http://www.100daysofrealfood.com/.

6 "Kraft: Stop Using Dangerous Food Dyes in Our Mac & Cheese." *Change.org*. Web. 4 September 2015. https://www.change.org/p/kraft-stop-using-dangerous-food-dyes-in-our-mac-cheese.

7 Yvette d'Entremont, "The 'Food Babe' Blogger Is Full of Shit." *Gawker*. 6 April 2015. Web. 4 September 2015. http://gawker.com/the-food-babe-blogger-is-full-of-shit-1694902226.

8 Meghan Lynch (2010) "Healthy Habits or Damaging Diets: An Exploratory Study of a Food Blogging Community." *Ecology of Food and Nutrition*: 316–35.

9 "Food Facts 2012: A BlogHer Study." *BlogHer Editors*. Web. 4 September 2015. http://www.blogher.com/food-facts-2012-blogher-study?page=full.

4

TRIPLE FOR A DOZEN

The rise and dominance of advocacy

> Politics has become much more advocacy based and, no matter what the issue is, you have to line up on the side of 'your group'. In essence, that means that people have already taken a position and we have missed something we used to talk about in public policy education, something we called the 'teachable moment' – when people were still considering the merits of an issue.
>
> *(Dr. Otto Doering, Professor of Agricultural Economics*
> *at Purdue University)*

The incredible, edible egg is a big deal. America's egg industry is larger than Guatemala's entire GDP. As of 2014, the average American ate 263 eggs every year[1]: less than one full egg a day, but significantly more than half an egg *every single day*. In July of 2015, annual egg production totaled $7.67 billion.[2]

California's consumers may be rethinking their egg consumption, however. Articles with headlines like "How California's New Rules Are Scrambling the Egg Industry,"[3] "Why Eggs Have Gotten More Expensive in California,"[4] and "Egg Prices Soar in California"[5] were pushed out by major national media in 2015. The explanation for the spike in the price of eggs is not just the avian influenza epidemic, nor the drought in California, but rather the reduction in stock by California's chicken farmers due to a new regulation on space requirements known as Proposition 2.

California's Proposition 2 was co-sponsored by the Humane Society and Farm Sanctuary (the biggest farm-animal rights group in the United States). They spearheaded what is known as a "ballot initiative." Ballot initiatives are a form of direct democracy available in 24 states where state-level initiatives can be put on the ballot. The process, which varies between states, requires a petition, a $200 fee, a review process, and collection of signatures, etc.[6] There are even a handful of California firms that make their livings by getting measures onto the ballot.

Ballot initiatives are a far cry from where they once were. Launched by reformers in the early twentieth century, they had hopes ballot initiatives would enable ordinary citizens to shape public policy and regain power. Today, as reported by the *Washington Post*, "The amount of cash spent rewriting state law through the initiative process has exploded in recent years, spawning a cottage industry of campaign consultants who make their living helping ideological groups and corporations alike qualify measures for the ballot."[7]

Proposition 2, a ballot initiative in California in 2008, required that animals be provided room to turn around, lie down, stand up, and fully extend their limbs. To most people, it sounded like a reasonable request. How, or even why, would someone want to argue against that point? To the non-agriculturalist, as stated, it appears perfectly acceptable and indeed even morally obligatory. Any negative ramifications to this decision were not, in any way, evident to the average consumer. Yet depending on their views and income, the average consumer may now find that the ramifications of such an initiative are, in fact, quite undesirable.

The spokeswoman for the leading anti-Proposition 2 group, Californians for Safe Food, tried to explain some of these consequences to the *New York Times* in 2008. "This is a well-intended initiative for animals with some very negative unintended consequences for people. It's going to wipe out the California egg farmers, and it's going to raise the food costs for consumers. And this is at a time when our economy is hurting."[8]

Wayne Pacelle, president and executive chief of the Humane Society, rebutted those concerns aggressively. In a blog post, he extolled an editorial[9] that had appeared in the *New York Times* supporting Proposition 2 with these lines, "The editorial writers didn't hedge about an extra penny-per-egg cost to shift from barren battery cages to cage-free housing systems. They didn't buy into the scare-mongering that any change in production systems means that all farmers will go out of business. They didn't buy into the false thinking that giant factory farms are good for rural communities." He also added that most people have developed a "multi-layered set of defenses and rationalizations to shield themselves from the harsh truth."[10]

In the end, over $15 million was spent in total advocating for and against this proposition. The Humane Society and their allies spent $8.73 million in support of Proposition 2 and those opposing it spent $7.38 million to try and prevent its passing.[11] On November 4, 2008, Proposition 2 did indeed pass, with 63.5 percent of voters in favor. Egg farmers and California consumers had seven years to prepare themselves for the change (other industries were not so heavily affected, as the chicken industry is the state's forte). DAIRY?

To put the $15 million spent on advocacy in perspective, that's the price of about 60 million eggs (with a dozen eggs priced at $3). There are about 40 million people[12] in California. Every Californian could have had one and a half free eggs. If prices were where they were *before* Proposition 2, everyone could have had about three free eggs.

What happened is one of the least socially optimal outcomes that can occur due to the lack of communication between advocates on different sides of food and agriculture issues. To put it bluntly, lawyers get rich, farmers go broke, and consumers pay higher prices. Imagine if the two competing parties could have found common ground on this issue and used the $15 million spent on lobbying efforts to transform California's egg industry into one that met desired animal welfare standards without wreaking havoc on farmers and jacking up prices for consumers.

It's possible that when it came time to actually implement these laws, many of the voters had long forgotten their cast ballots and were somewhat surprised when egg prices started to skyrocket. Yet agriculture could not forget. Between 2008 and 2015, there ensued a curious process in which California egg farmers had to ask for clarity on what it meant for a chicken to be able to "extend its limbs fully and turn around freely." To make sure they were in compliance with the law, they needed to know exactly what it meant and the verbiage on Proposition 2 was far too broad for any type of application. The California Department of Food and Agriculture eventually ruled that 116 square inches would be appropriate, so long as there are nine birds or more in the same cage.[13]

At the time of the bill passing in 2008, voters didn't know that egg demand would have grown by 2015 when the bill was implemented (due to soaring meat prices that caused Americans to turn to other protein sources). The poorest consumers are the hardest hit. They are already on a tight budget, and eggs are traditionally the cheap source of protein. Also, many egg farmers, in attempts to meet the 116 square inch regulation, turned to 'cage-free' open pens for eggs. Cage free can be good, but not all cage free is created equal. University of California at Davis researcher Frank Mitloehner highlighted some concerns about large cage-free flocks, listing amongst other animal welfare issues the "high incidence of cannibalism in cage-free systems, and also high incidence of bone breakage."[14]

Beyond providing space for chickens to spread their wings, Proposition 2 had additional consequences. While many Californians have peace of mind knowing that their chickens have enough space to do the hokey-pokey and turn themselves around, there are other Californians who can't afford this type of peace of mind. The spike in egg prices creates the largest budgetary strain for California's lowest wage earners. To the truly poor, a dollar or two extra per dozen really does impact the weekly budget. In addition, many egg farmers suffered trying to comply. It is possible that while many citizens wanted safer conditions for animals, they were also *not* comfortable putting a number of farmers out of business and raising food prices on the poor during tough times.

Our new political world is centered around advocacy. People find their position, push their cause, and surround themselves with like-minded peers. Advocacy is not intrinsically bad, but it can often create an information petri dish – only one tiny segment of the debate is being looked at under the microscope. Our current advocacy culture can often push one issue to the extreme. We need to be aware of its drawbacks and when it neglects to inform us of the bigger picture. Advocacy taken to the extreme does not promote dialogue; rather, it creates a shouting match between two groups intent on drowning out the other's voice.

If the contending parties in this conflict could have engaged in a conversation, or perhaps been forced to by consumer demand, would it have been possible to create a more elegant solution? Could the $15 million spent on advocacy have been used to create a space for a productive dialogue? In an advocacy-only environment, there is little space for the type of communication that brings different perspectives to the table. The results of this type of environment are sub-par policies that do not reflect the excellence we are capable of. It is possible to contend with varying needs and demands, but only through communication.

Notes

1 "Welcome to the American Egg Board – Industry Overview" (n.d.). Retrieved September 20, 2015, from http://www.aeb.org/farmers-and-marketers/industry-overview.
2 "Chickens and Eggs" (2015, August 21). Retrieved September 20, 2015, from http://usda.mannlib.cornell.edu/usda/nass/ChicEggs//2010s/2015/ChicEggs-08-21-2015.pdf.
3 "How California's New Rules Are Scrambling the Egg Industry" (2014, December 29). Retrieved September 20, 2015, from http://www.npr.org/sections/thesalt/2014/12/29/373802858/how-californias-new-rules-are-scrambling-the-egg-industry.
4 "Why Eggs Have Gotten More Expensive in California" (2015, June 18). Retrieved September 20, 2015, from http://www.latimes.com/food/dailydish/la-dd-eggs-prices-expensive-california-20150617-story.html.
5 "Egg Prices Soar in California" (2015, August 24). Retrieved September 20, 2015, from http://www.nbcsandiego.com/news/local/Egg-Prices-Soar-in-California--322707371.html.
6 "Laws Governing the Initiative Process in California – Ballotpedia" (n.d.). Retrieved September 21, 2015, from https://ballotpedia.org/Laws_governing_the_initiative_process_in_California.

7   R. Wilson (2013, November 8) "Initiative Spending Booms Past $1 Billion as Corporations Sponsor Their Own Proposals," *Washington Post*. Retrieved September 21, 2015, from http://www.washingtonpost. com/blogs/govbeat/wp/2013/11/08/initiative-spending-booms-past-1-billion-as-corporations-sponsor-their-own-proposals/.

 8   J. Mckinley (2008, October 23). "A California Ballot Measure Offers Rights for Farm Animals." Retrieved September 21, 2015, from http:// www.nytimes.com/2008/10/24/us/24egg.html.

 9   "Standing, Stretching, Turning Around" (2008, October 8). Retrieved September 21, 2015, from http://www.nytimes.com/2008/10/09/ opinion/09thu3.html.

10   "Proposition 2: Views Fit to Print – A Humane Nation" (2008, October 9). Retrieved September 21, 2015, from http://blog. humanesociety.org/wayne/2008/10/prop2-nytimes.html?credit=blog _post_100908_id5361.

11   "PROPOSITION 002," FollowTheMoney.org (n.d.). Retrieved September 21, 2015, from http://www.followthemoney.org/ entity-details?eid=10246623.

12   "California QuickFacts from the US Census Bureau" (n.d.). Retrieved September 24, 2015, from http://quickfacts.census.gov/qfd/states/ 06000.html.

13   "New Shell Egg Food Safety Regulations" (n.d.). Retrieved November 18, 2015, from http://ucanr.edu/sites/CESonomaAgOmbuds/files/ 174478.pdf.

14   A. Westervelt (2015, March 2). "The Unintended Consequences of California's Chicken Cage Law." Retrieved September 21, 2015, from http://www.theguardian.com/sustainable-business/food-blog/2015/ mar/02/california-egg-law-cage-free-pasture.

5

TECHNICAL DIFFICULTIES

Grappling with the benefits and risks of GMOs

Obviously we haven't been able to communicate this [GMOs] efficiently so that a large number of Americans can cease having anxiety about the food that they're eating. I'm in favor of there being very, very tough scientific scrutiny of our food supply. But the results of this have got to be pushed out ... they [consumers] need much greater knowledge about how food is produced in this country.

(Senator Richard Lugar)

A simple online search engine query asking, "What are GMOs?" yields a wealth of responses, of which precious few originate from neutral sources. The first to appear in a standard Google search of this question is the Non-GMO Project's definition, followed by a slew of other media outlets staking out their own interpretation. On the first page of search results, *USA Today* boasts a "What You Need to Know about GMOs" Q&A written by a journalist who specializes in multimedia.[1] *Daily Finance* displays "10 Foods You'll Have to Give Up to Avoid Eating GMOs," with a dubious historical interpretation of GMOs by way of introduction.[2]

Google shows ten search listings per page. Traffic, the number of people who click on a search result, drops off by 95 percent by the second page of Google search results.[3] Those first ten results that pop up in a search get the lion's share of views, and searches for "GMOs" have quintupled on Google since 2012.[4] This means that when someone, anyone, decides to research GMOs and they type it into their Google search engine, they are extremely likely to only glance through the first few search hits that pop up – those that are described above.

The most popular online search engine image for GMOs is a tomato with a syringe sticking out of it. Other popular images to appear are fruits cut in half with unexpected insides. Rather than finding the flesh of an apple inside the outline of an apple, one finds a kiwi, an orange, or even, in one disturbing case, the outline of an actual human fetus.[5] To someone with no knowledge of what GMOs are, these images are nefarious and disturbing. When confronted with such an overwhelming flood of images conveying the same chilling, nebulous, vague kind of 'idea,' it is only natural to start developing a negative bias toward GMOs without having gotten any real scientific knowledge or understanding.

What *are* they, then? Genetically modified organisms are by definition organisms whose genetic material has been altered by means of genetic engineering.[6] To genetically engineer is to change the genetic makeup of cells. In traditional plant breeding, this is achieved by crossing two plants that have desirable traits to attain an outcome with a mix of traits. Through genetic modification, scientists can introduce one singular and specific desirable trait, and this trait may be introduced from a different species. Traits that were previously difficult or impossible to breed are now done with relative ease.

This may still seem like a cryptic definition to non-geneticists, which is most of us. It's quite common that people don't actually fully comprehend what 'genetic material' is or what 'genetic engineering' means. Genetic engineering is not a simple concept, as we saw earlier, and it can encompass a wide array of practices: better controlling weeds or pests, enhancing quality traits to improve nutrient content, contributing to pharmaceutical or industrial purposes. 'Golden rice' is one example where a crop's nutritional content is enhanced. This crop was developed with increased amounts of vitamin A in order to prevent childhood blindness and death in underdeveloped countries.[7]

Current media headlines regarding GMOs fail to appreciate the complexity of the issue: "Erin Brockovich: The Biotech Industry Is Jeopardizing Our Health – Consumers must demand labels on Genetically Modified Organisms" in *Time*,[8] "Christie Brinkley on GMOs: 'We're Guinea Pigs'" in *FOX Business*,[9] "Girl Scouts' Science-Based GMO Stance Worth Cookies' Dollar Price Increase" in *Forbes*.[10] The issue of GMOs has become a hot-button topic in today's media. The latest 'take' on GMOs floods in from every direction; blogs, social media, friends, and marketers. However, as the sampling of headlines indicates, we are often hearing this 'take' from people with no scientific background on the matter.

GMOs are a prevalent issue in our society, and the natural response to a popular issue is for people to try to formulate their own opinion. Are GMOs okay, or aren't they? While critics of GMOs have public opinion on their side, they don't have the corpus of factual information and scientific conclusions. Yet despite this, they have had incredible influence on the public debate. It has even become trendy to dislike GMOs. *Medical Daily* reported, "Why People Say No to GMO: Popular Psychology and Ethics, Not Science, Spur Dislike." The article gets to the root of the matter, noting that despite the fact that "many people do not even know what GMO stands for, never mind what the products do, the idea of GMOs is often met with vehement disapproval."[11]

The report cites a study that explains how anti-GMO campaigns tap into human emotions such as morality and disgust, and that, once tapped, these emotions are extremely difficult to counter.[12] Lead author of the study Stefaan Blancke also explained in a press release that "For a very long time people have been only hearing one side. Scientists aren't generally involved with the public understanding of GMOs."[13] Those who are anti-GMO have been operating for quite some time without a strong counter-argument.

The fate of this issue, more so than any other, comes down to a battle of public opinion. Scientific consensus concludes that GMOs are safe for consumption[14] and result in positive economic outcomes,[15] but consumer opinion is not so monolithic. A PEW poll comparing discrepancies between general scientific opinion and consumer perception ranked GMO safety for human health as having the largest gap.[16] It wins the dubious award of having the biggest discrepancy between scientific and public opinion of any scientific issue today.

On a global scale, opinions on GMOs are divided and regulations on crop cultivation, seed development, and imports vary. The United States, Brazil, Argentina, India, and Canada allow the planting and sale of GM crops; others do not. In China, only certain varieties can be cultivated. Much of Europe has rejected domestic cultivation of GMOs and requires labeling of any product that contains ingredients that were genetically modified. They're following the "precautionary principle" that a new technology can be blocked simply on suspicion of a risk not yet tested for, or because a risk not found in the short run might nonetheless develop in the long run.[17] Even within countries such as the United States, differences in opinion on the acceptability of GMO technology differ across application and use. For instance, medical applications and non-agri-food technologies, such as cotton, are more acceptable than those used in food.

During our research and interviews, it became increasingly clear that this is one of the, if not *the*, most challenging communications issues confronting food and agriculture today. And the fate of the issue rests on how and what is communicated – not the factual reality. It is tempting to respond by trying to continue to talk 'science' to the public; however, research shows that this is unlikely to result in consumer acceptance.[18] Prior belief about the technology is the largest determining factor in perception of GMOs, and at this point in the debate many people have formed their opinions.

In the article "Consumer Acceptance of New Food Technologies: Causes and Roots of Controversies," the authors explained that "when consumers received, from major scientific bodies, 'objective' information (e.g., that currently approved GM foods were safe to eat) that conflicted with their prior beliefs, they often chose to ignore the new information or even to double down on their prior beliefs (e.g., saying that they were now more concerned about the safety of eating GM food than they were before) rather than adjusting their beliefs to coincide with the new information."[19] It does *not* follow, however, that because 'objective' and 'new' information doesn't always work, the absence of it will alleviate the problem. A void of information often provokes consumers to adopt a self-protective attitude based on suspicion and fear.

What does this mean? Does this mean that there's no hope for a healthy conversation around GMOs? No, it does not. It highlights the importance of understanding public perception and responding with strategic communication. When new information is presented to the public – tossed out in an ad hoc manner and patched together based on loose assumptions of what the public *should* know (not what they want to know) – it often falls flat. People don't listen to what you think is important; they listen to what they think is important.

What are the issues surrounding genetically modified products that influence consumers, and why are they altering public perception to the negative? Food safety, environmental damage, fear, and the ethical concern of "tampering with nature" all come into play in people's decisions to oppose GMOs. Segments of the public also view GMOs as a form of corporate domination over helpless farmers, even though farmers commonly choose to use them because they can reduce inputs and costs. In this environment, it is difficult to share the positive – that peer reviewed scientific journals point to the overwhelming positive benefits of GMOs. This is true across agronomy, biology, public health, and economic journals. GMO crops result in positive economic outcomes even for the poorest people, as well as reducing pesticide and herbicide use,[20] in addition to being safe for human consumption.[21]

The broad message blasted across agriculture about 'global food security' does not address the specific questions and concerns confronting consumers. *Feeding the world*, as per the pro-GMO message, may not be the appropriate soundbite given its simplicity in the face of a complex issue – and it doesn't necessarily reflect the moral attitudes and beliefs of the broad consumer base today. Consumer concerns can be broken down into much smaller pieces: the future, nutrition, their livelihood, their communities. There is GMO-specific research happening in these areas, and an increased focus on more subtle messages could be more persuasive in helping consumers understand the realities of GMOs and their potential impact.

Where positive stories are evident and documented, negative rhetoric can overwhelm them. Often information about GMOs is presented in non-scientific venues where it can be very easy to 'claim' and 'summarize' what science purports, in such a way that the true meaning has been distorted beyond recognition. Similar to a subject like climate change, it's easy to generate propaganda that climate science just 'isn't there' or 'there isn't enough evidence' when quite the opposite is true. The public doesn't commonly assess their sources, and they need to. Even this can be used as a starting place for conversations about the objective facts on GMOs.

As with any new technology, society must look at the pros and cons and assess the balance. Public assessment of risk is a factor that consistently undermines the GMO conversation. Different factors come into play when gauging risk, and we look at this in more depth in a later chapter, and it plays a big role in conversations on GMOs. In an interview, Dr. Jayson Lusk, Regents Professor and Willard Sparks Endowed Chair in the Department of Agricultural Economics at Oklahoma State University, as well as author of *The Food Police* and *Compassion, by the Pound*, provided one example to illustrate this point: when we drive a car we are in control and therefore don't perceive it to be a risky act; of course, it's one of the riskier things most of us will ever do. Consumers feel out of control over a farmer's decision to use GMOs and so they automatically appear risky. Unfamiliarity with the real risks can stimulate a sense of dread.

The manner in which GMOs were introduced plays a role in today's public understanding. In the United States, when the regulatory framework for the matter was being developed, there was little interest in the issue in Congress. There was, however, a debate between two outlooks: one that only wanted to regulate the *product*, the other that wanted to regulate the *process*. It was eventually concluded that the product was what was subject to regulation, and this has been the basis for policy since. Later, the Food and Drug Administration determined that labeling was not required on the basis of the method of food production, but only if the new food itself posed safety problems for consumers.[22] Rejection of labeling and a lack of abundant, reliable information create an environment that fosters a sense of helplessness in the face of overwhelming 'powers.'

Public trust in experts and institutions is important.[23] The public doesn't always trust institutional assessment of risk in the case of GMOs.[24][25] And the issue of trust and source is just one more hurdle that will have to be overcome if the public is going to understand the real risks and benefits of GMOs. Communication on this issue is not only important, it is crucial. Efforts have demonstrated that even when institutions have communicated factual information about the risks and benefits of food technologies, a consumer may not be willing to accept them. Regulatory institutions will need to reassess their approach – but they first need to work on being trusted. Once trust is established, the public's concerns must be heard and accommodated. Communication will need to be structured in a way that can address the public's concerns, no matter how real or how irrational those concerns may be.

The obstacle for GMOs is communication; trust, transparency, addressed concerns, messages that resonate. Public acceptance will determine whether GM technology moves forward or not.[26] It boils down to the most basic economic concept – supply and demand. If consumers demand non-GMO products either through regulation or by demonstrating with their buying behavior that they will pay a premium for them, then the markets will meet their requests. Communication around GMOs requires one of the most important, yet most underrated, elements of communication – listening. The only way to understand the public's perceptions of GMOs, and the values that dictate these perceptions, is to listen carefully to what really worries them and respond in kind.

Notes

1   J. Network (2014, January 3) "What You Need to Know about GMOs." Retrieved December 4, 2015, from http://www.usatoday.com/story/news/nation-now/2014/01/03/gmo-genetically-modified-organism-facts-cheerios/4302121/.

2   B. Stoffel (2013, November 21) "10 Foods You'll Have to Give Up to Avoid Eating GMOs," *DailyFinance*. Retrieved December 4, 2015, from http://www.dailyfinance.com/2013/11/21/foods-give-up-avoid-eating-gmo/.

3   J. Lee (2013, June 20) "No. 1 Position in Google Gets 33% of Search Traffic [Study]." Retrieved December 4, 2015, from http://searchenginewatch.com/sew/study/2276184/no-1-position-in-google-gets-33-of-search-traffic-study#.

4   "Google Trends – Web Search interest – Worldwide, 2004–present" (n.d.). Retrieved December 4, 2015, from https://www.google.com/trends/explore#q=GMOs.

5   "GMOs," Google Search (n.d.). Retrieved December 4, 2015, from https://www.google.com/search?q=GMOs&espv=2&biw=1920&bih=1075&source=lnms&tbm=isch&sa=X&ved=0ahUKEwj28J_I9MLJAhWiioMKHZL7C4wQ_AUIBygC#imgrc=yRaxrh00zEioxM.

6   (N.d.). Retrieved December 2, 2015, from http://dictionary.reference.com/browse/gmo.

7   "Golden Rice Project" (n.d.). Retrieved December 2, 2015, from http://www.goldenrice.org/.

8   "Erin Brockovich: The Biotech Industry Is Jeopardizing Our Health." *Time*. 1 December 2015. Web. 3 December 2015. http://time.com/4129785/erin-brockovich-gmos/.

9   Jade Scipioni, "Christie Brinkley on GMOS: 'We're Guinea Pigs'." *FOX Business*. 17 November 2015. Web. 3 December 2015. http://www.foxbusiness.com/business-leaders/2015/11/17/christie-brinkley-on-gmos-were-guinea-pigs/.

10 Kavin Senapathy, "Girl Scouts' Science-Based GMO Stance Worth Cookies' Dollar Increase." *Forbes*. Forbes Magazine, 12 November 2015. Web. 3 December 2015. http://www.forbes.com/sites/kavinsenapathy/2015/11/12/girl-scouts-science-based-stance-worth-dollar-price-increase/.

11 Dana Dovey, "Why People Say No to GMO: Popular Psychology and Ethics, Not Science, Spur Dislike." *Medical Daily*. 28 April 2015. Web. 3 December 2015. http://www.medicaldaily.com/why-people-say-no-gmo-popular-psychology-and-ethics-not-science-spur-dislike-331126.

12 Stefaan Blancke, Frank Van Breusegem, Geert De Jaeger, Johan Braeckman, and Marc Van Montagu (2015) "Fatal Attraction: The Intuitive Appeal of GMO Opposition," *Trends in Plant Science*,20(7): 414–418.

13 "The Appeal of Being Anti-GMO," *CELL PRESS*. 24 April 2015. Web. 3 December 2015. http://www.eurekalert.org/pub_releases/2015-04/cp-tao042415.php.

14 "Statement by the AAAS Board of Directors on Labeling of Genetically Modified Foods" (n.d.). Retrieved December 2, 2015, from http://www.aaas.org/news/statement-aaas-board-directors-labeling-genetically-modified-foods.

15 W. Klümper and M. Qaim (2014) "A Meta-analysis of the Impacts of Genetically Modified Crops," *PLoS One*, 9(11): e111629.
16 http://www.pewinternet.org/2015/01/29/chapter-3-attitudes-and-beliefs-on-science-and-technology-topics/.
17 Joyce Tait (2001) "More Faust than Frankenstein: The European Debate about the Precautionary Principle and Risk Regulation for Genetically Modified Crops," *Journal of Risk Research*, 1(4): 175–189.
18 L. Frewer, J. Lassen, B. Kettlitz, J. Scholderer, V. Beekman and K. Berdal (n.d.). "Societal Aspects of Genetically Modified Foods," *Food and Chemical Toxicology*, 42(7): 1181–1193.
19 J. Lusk, J. Roosen and A. Bieberstein (2014) "Consumer Acceptance of New Food Technologies: Causes and Roots of Controversies," *Annual Review of Resource Economics*, 6(1): 381–405.
20 M. Qaim (2009) "The Economics of Genetically Modified Crops," *Annual Review of Resource Economics*, 1(1): 665–694.
21 T. A. Hemphill and S. Banerjee (2015) "Genetically Modified Organisms and the US Retail Food Labeling Controversy: Consumer Perceptions, Regulation, and Public Policy," *Business and Society Review*, 120(3): 435–464.
22 D. Lynch and D. Vogel (2001, April 5) "The Regulation of GMOs in Europe and the United States: A Case-Study of Contemporary European Regulatory Politics." Retrieved December 4, 2015, from http://www.cfr.org/agricultural-policy/regulation-gmos-europe-united-states-case-study-contemporary-european-regulatory-politics/p8688.
23 J. R. Eiser, S. Miles, and L. J. Frewer (2002) "Trust, Perceived Risk, and Attitudes toward Food Technologies," *Journal of Applied Social Psychology*, 32(11): 2423–2433.
24 M. L. Finucane (2002) "Mad Cows, Mad Corn and Mad Communities: The Role of Socio-cultural Factors in the Perceived Risk of Genetically-modified Food," *Proceedings of the Nutrition Society*, 61(1): 31–37.
25 L. Frewer, J. Lassen, B. Kettlitz, J. Scholderer, V. Beekman and K. Berdal (n.d.). "Societal Aspects of Genetically Modified Foods," *Food and Chemical Toxicology*, 42(7): 1181–1193.
26 M. Costa-Font, J. Gil and W. Traill (2008) "Consumer Acceptance, Valuation of and Attitudes towards Genetically Modified Food: Review and Implications for Food Policy," *Food Policy*, 33(2): 99–111.

PART II

The nuances

A number of themes underscore many of our food and agricultural conversations. Drawing upon Part I as well as introducing new examples, Part II contains four chapters that delve deeply into the nuances of these overarching challenges. After each chapter in this section, a stakeholder from different segments of the agricultural dialogue expresses their perspective through a Q&A or short essay. These guest voices – a consumer, farmer, policymaker, and academic – provide outlooks and viewpoints on food and agricultural communications that could only be conveyed through their unique experiences.

6

EMOTIONS AND AGRICULTURE

> We in agriculture love to talk about safe, abundant and affordable food. … We're talking about it in economic terms, we're talking about it in scientific terms – and they're looking for an answer that acknowledges their right to be concerned and expresses sympathy for them as consumers.
>
> *(Chris Novak, CEO of the National Corn Growers Association)*

"The Worst Mistake in the History of the Human Race"[1] was the headline of a *Discover Magazine* article from 1987 by Jared Diamond. A chilling headline, eliciting images of warfare, slavery, genocide. Yet the somewhat startling subject of this article? Agriculture. Over twenty years later, Sanjida O'Connell wrote in the *Telegraph*, a well-known and high-circulation British newspaper, "Could it be that rather than being a boon to mankind, the invention of agriculture was, in the words of one academic, 'the worst mistake in human history'?"[2] Yet another article, in the *Ecologist* in 2006, concluded: "Humanity's Worst Invention: Agriculture."[3]

These are extreme examples, but they underscore a trend. As the years have passed, consumers and the general public have been hearing increasingly disturbing reports about our food system. The conversation has migrated from the fringe to the center, and it's no wonder that the average person has become, at best, skeptical of how their food is made. Consumers want to make the best decision for their health and the environment, and the only way most people know how to affect change is to make what they consider ethical purchases based on the soundbites they've picked up along the way. Consumers, concerned with ethics, face dilemma after dilemma: Which of these cuts of beef came from ethically treated cows? Which brand of coffee is fair-trade? When every purchase carries moral weight, it can be overwhelming and challenging to make decisions that align with values.

Consumers are critical players in today's agricultural conversations. To communicate effectively with consumers means to understand them. Messages are conveyed effectively when we understand our audience's or receiver's outlook, comprehension, and situation. Understanding does not mean agreement, nor does it imply an acceptance or approval of a view or outlook. Yet it gives the bigger picture so we can correct our communication approaches and ensure we're barking up the right tree. As sociologist Dr. Janet Ayres said, "We are not born competent communicators. We have to learn how to communicate well and we do this through awareness, experience and reflecting on what works well and what doesn't work well."

Consumers are important because they are getting involved, they're asking for change, and they're driving the demand for how companies conduct their businesses. Consumers have increasing power over what companies produce, and in turn what these companies request of agriculture. Sixty major global food retailers, including McDonald's, Kraft Foods, Kroger, Costco, and Burger King, have agreed to stop sourcing meat from producers that use gestation crates,[4] a practice that was highly scrutinized by animal welfare groups. Restaurants and major suppliers, including McDonald's, Chick-fil-A, Tyson Foods, and Perdue are reducing or eliminating the use of chickens treated with antibiotics.[5] The National Resource Defense Council even estimated that one-third of the entire US chicken industry already has committed to discontinuing the use of routine use of antibiotics in meat.[6] This change is almost entirely rooted in a grass-roots movements.

In addition, many people are engaging in the 'Food Movement,' which encourages social and cultural change in the food system. The starting point of the movement varies depending on who you talk to and what you're talking about (slow food, local food, sustainable food, raw food, or any other of the multitude of connected movements) but it's largely agreed that the food movement kicked off in the 1970s and 1980s with a focus on the environment (after Rachel Carson's *Silent Spring* spurred the closely related environmental movement).

The 'Food Movement,' in a nutshell, denotes the many people across the nation who are becoming or already are passionately engaged or interested in their food and where it comes from. These people are interested in how the food-supply chain works, and how the food we eat gets from farm to table. The food movement looks at and attempts to critique or influence the way we eat. Michael Pollan, an author and well-known driver of the food movement, has a bold take on its appeal: "What is attracting so many people to the movement today (and young people in particular) is a much less conventional kind of politics, one that is about something more than food. The food movement is also about community, identity, pleasure, and, most notably, about carving out a new social and economic space removed from the influence of big corporations on the one side and government on the other."[7]

Pollan's words could be understood to mean that being a part of the food movement is comparable to stating that you belong to a political party. This is a somewhat audacious, perhaps even questionable, statement – but one that highlights the ambitions and drive of those behind the movement. Understanding the drive behind the movement, and what comprises it, is crucial background information necessary for understanding what consumers face in terms of societal trends and attitudes.

The US Farmers & Ranchers Alliance Consumer Survey reported that 70 percent of consumers said their purchase decisions were affected by how food was grown and raised, and three-quarters said they think about this topic while grocery shopping.[8] Yet according to the Chicago Council for Global Affairs, the majority of Americans name affordability and nutrition as the most important factor in their decision-making. They stated, "There is a growing interest in food in the United States: where it comes from, how it is made, and what it represents ... Contrary to the visibility of the debate about GMOs, antibiotics, and local food, the vast majority of Americans value food that is above all affordable, safe, and nutritious."[9] Why the disconnect?

It can be partially explained by the fact that food in the United States is already relatively safe and inexpensive. Many Americans have more flexibility in their budgets for food than ever before. In 1960 Americans spent almost 18 percent of their disposable income on food; today they spend less than 10 percent on food.[10] As top concerns for consumers are already largely being met, there is a freedom that was historically not available to delve deeper into food issues, to ponder how food was grown and raised, and to think about these matters while waiting to check out. Consumers are *not* wrong for doing this; it is the fundamental right of the consumer to question.

Part of the frustration in responding to consumers on these matters is that vocal minorities tend to get the lion's share of media attention and airtime. Vocal minorities don't always reflect the concerns of the majority – which is often a moderate, reasonable stance. Just as we see in our political discussions, public debate is commonly out of sync with actual American interest.

Many current agricultural messages do not resonate with consumers nor assuage their concerns. They often speak to the issue, not the person. While parts of agriculture struggle to hit that emotional chord, other voices don't. Marketers, advocacy groups, bloggers, and celebrities 'get' the emotional tug of food and health, a feelings-charged topic. The link between these two is a powerful catalyst for emotion.

Jolene Brown, a farmer and professional speaker, explained, "Always remember, the value is in the eyes of the consumer, not the creator; the purchaser not the producer. And today's consumers are valuing five things: time, youth, safety, health, and an experience. Linking what you do with words and actions that provide those things takes you beyond educating to building a relationship." Health is linked to food, and food is linked to agriculture. Health issues are emotional, not least the issue of obesity. This is one of the most prevalent emotional trigger issues because it not only affects a person's health but their social status as well. Overweight people are highly stigmatized[11] and weight discrimination is on the rise, having increased dramatically in recent years in the United States.[12] Obese people have fewer opportunities in the workplace and in education.[13] When the term obesity gets caught up in the debate surrounding "natural" foods, this powerful emotional trigger word makes it hard to make an intellectual decision.

In the 2012 Food & Health Survey conducted by the International Food Information Council Foundation, half of those polled believed it is easier to do their taxes than to figure out how to eat healthfully.[14] Given how stress-inducing and byzantine our tax system is, that anyone – let alone half of those surveyed – would find it easier than eating well is about as much indication as we need that navigating food is hard. Labeling can add to this confusion. There is a USDA program that oversees the use of the term "organic." However, there is no set standard for the use of the term "natural." "Organic" is a category of food defined by federal law; "natural" is a meaningless marketing term. Yet are the meanings of the two terms all that different to the average consumer? Do they really know which one is governed by law and which isn't?

In addition, food itself is innately emotional. Eating activates neural substrates in many of the same ways abuse drugs can.[15] Food choices, the quantity, and the frequency of meals are all dependent on many variables. These variables often are not necessarily related to our physiological needs.[16] There's a reason your favorite meal from childhood is called "comfort" food. Think about your favorite holidays. You're emotionally attached to the dishes you serve on those days. The tradition and the memories that go into baking your green bean casserole are just as important as the ingredients you use. Threaten to take away someone's Thanksgiving turkey, and that may be the last threat you ever make.

Animal welfare is another strong emotional trigger for consumers. Livestock, and animals in general, have the potential to evoke strong feelings. They're often seen as helpless, subjected to the cruel whims of their farmer overseers. One farmer we spoke with claimed that pets have been elevated to familial status while livestock have been elevated to pet status. Additionally, ethical guidelines *widely* vary. For most, there is a fundamental difference between raising and killing animals to feed a country (or a single family, for that matter) and strangling your pet cat. Yet for some, there isn't, and for others the boundaries are becoming increasingly blurred as miscommunications around the matter grow. Communicating about an emotional issue requires special care and attention. In the book *Compassion, by the Pound: The Economics of Farm Animal Welfare*, the authors accept that "writing about animal welfare is a bit like writing about politics or religion – it is virtually impossible to keep from offending the reader."[17]

The food and agriculture industry is complex and can be extremely confusing to the average consumer. Agriculture uses a lot of terminology that's difficult to relate to. These terms may be unfamiliar or even sound unnatural. To even put food and technology in the same sentence can throw someone off kilter. The journal article "Consumer Acceptance of New Food Technologies: Causes and Roots of Controversies"[18] discusses the hardwired human evolutionary element to ward against new and unfamiliar foods. For centuries it was ingrained in humans to beware a seemingly harmless but unfamiliar berry or mushroom because it might kill. Technologies used commonly in agriculture or food processing simply sound like something to avoid – pesticides seem nonessential to a person who has never had to battle with pests and weeds.

Then there's the issue of hormones. They *sound* bad. That's what baseball players use to cheat, and what meatheads use in the gym to augment their bodies. The term carries tons of baggage in our society. It's associated with fakeness, cheating, lying. But this shows a misunderstanding of hormones' specialized use in the agricultural industry. There is a certain affinity for terms like "organic" and "non-GMO" because we tend to prefer food that is associated with language that makes it seem more natural or pure. Technological developments that have been transformative to the industry, cow-milking robots and precision nutrient application technologies, are unlikely to ignite much excitement and are hard to understand. So these technological innovations – innovations that make our food safer and cheaper – aren't likely to be included in the public rhetoric.

Incomplete knowledge or overly complex information causes people to rely on their emotional responses even more.[19] Determining what is fact, and what isn't, can be a difficult maze to navigate. Information presented by advertisers is often inaccurate or misleading, yet in our current communication climate it's the easiest information to access. In agriculture, many things are done out of sight (and therefore out of mind), so the industry may not appear to be very transparent and many issues remain confusing. Chris Waldrop, Director at Consumer Federation of America, talked with us at length about this issue from the perspective of consumers:

> There's a need for a lot more transparency and open discussion and explanation of why farmers and agriculture are making the decisions they are making. I think that a lot of times there are things that are hidden because the food system is very complex and there are a lot of decisions being made at a lot of different points. But with some of the decisions, if you can talk to consumers in a way that is honest and open, and say "here's why I use antibiotics" or "here's how I use them," "here's why I spray pesticides" or "here's why I use genetically modified seeds to plant," "here are the benefits to me and here's why I find value of doing this action" – at least consumers would then have a better understanding of what the decisions are and why they are being made. Right now there's a lot of skepticism among consumers about the agricultural industry and the things they do, because a lot of it is behind closed doors. In some regard, because they hear about pesticide residues, they hear about GMOs, or they hear about use of antibiotics – and it doesn't sound like something that they want to support – the consumers immediately say, "I don't want that." They may still say "I don't want that" even if you're being open and transparent about it, but that dialogue is missing a little bit in terms of explaining and understanding the reasons behind those sides and trying to explain why those sides have their perspectives.

With a somewhat different perspective, Dr. Jayson Lusk considers consumer ignorance of agriculture and our food supply:

> We don't know many things about a great deal of the products we regularly buy and consume. How is your iPhone made? How does Wi-Fi work? The fact that we know next to nothing about these issues doesn't keep us from enjoying them. In fact, one of the reasons people know so little about production agriculture is because technologies have been developed that have made farmers so incredibly productive, we now need many fewer farmers than in the past. In general, that's a good thing because it's freed us up to do other enjoyable things in life. The downside is that when we lack a connection with food and agriculture and the ability to check the things we hear and read on the internet with the "facts on the ground," the potential arises for our beliefs about food and agriculture to be disconnected from reality.[20]

Lusk's thoughtful answer is a valuable perspective on the subject. Yet in the words of Dr. Ken Foster, Professor and Head of the Department of Agricultural Economics at Purdue University, "We don't eat our iPhones, and that alters our interest in the technological details." Lusk is right, though – it's extremely difficult for the everyday consumer to understand the intricacies of caring for and harvesting livestock and complex soil systems, let alone the economics behind ensuring that people at home and abroad have secure livelihoods while also maintaining access to safe and affordable food. We can't all be experts on everything. Yet, as he concluded, the downside of this technological shift is people's inability to check the "facts on the ground." If a critical mass of people don't understand how agriculture works and are making their decisions based on emotions, they may advocate for things that aren't actually in line with their preferences. They may distrust and discount the views of players who have knowledge and experience as biased or cynical tools of "big ag."

Indeed, it is hard. Chuck Conner laments: "Problems we encounter? It is far more difficult and takes far more time and far more words to explain factual information versus the soundbite snippets of, 'You're eating that and it's going to kill you' – the message on the other side. Ours is, 'here is all this information, all of these studies, all of these university analyses.' Ours requires more time. We live in an instantaneous kind of society, where their information comes from one click of a button and then they move on."

What can also make understanding the consumer perspective so hard, so often, is that discussions that surround agriculture are very sensitive for those actually working in agriculture. Farming can be a way of life, a vocation. In some cases the farm employs multiple members of the family. Many farmers and ranchers inherited their land from generations before them. It permeates so much of their lives and they become emotionally attached to their profession. There's the burden of stress from investing so much financially into the expensive assets required to run a farm, and Mother Nature is an unpredictable and humbling force. Farmers can also have emotional responses to heated conversations and touchy communication situations. In today's climate, it is common for a farmer to be attacked for their profession (which for many farmers is their very identity), and this can create an environment where communication shuts down entirely, or spirals rapidly out of control. It's extremely hard to empathize when someone feels attacked, demeaned, or disrespected.

Like any complex area, agricultural decisions often rest on the nuances, and to understand these requires access to the education and information that would allow consumers to take a more nuanced approach. Yet despite the challenges of communicating technicalities, the intricacies of navigating emotion, and the plain old hard work that it takes to listen proactively, there is no other option if we want to improve the dialogue around food and agriculture. Consumers are sending a resoundingly loud message – they are interested, and they will be and they are a part of the conversation. The first step in improving communications is understanding this, and trying to understand them.

Notes

1 J. Diamond (1987, May 1) "The Worst Mistake in the History of the Human Race." Retrieved January 7, 2016, from http://discovermagazine.com/1987/may/02-the-worst-mistake-in-the-history-of-the-human-race.

2 S. O'Connell (2009, June 23) "Is Farming the Root of All Evil?" Retrieved January 7, 2016, from http://www.telegraph.co.uk/news/science/science-news/5604296/Is-farming-the-root-of-all-evil.html.

3 C. Dennis (2006, September 26) "Humanity's Worst Invention: Agriculture." Retrieved January 7, 2016, from http://www.theecologist.org/investigations/food_and_farming/268902/humanitys_worst_invention_agriculture.html.

4 "Food Company Policies on Gestation Crates" (n.d.). Retrieved January 5, 2016, from http://cratefreefuture.com/pdf/Gestation%20Crate%20Elimination%20Policies.pdf.

5 P. Huffstutter (2015, April 28) "Tyson Foods to End Use of Human Antibiotics in U.S. Chickens by 2017." Retrieved January 5, 2016, from http://www.reuters.com/article/us-tyson-foods-antibiotics-id USKBN0NJ0TA20150428.

6 "Going Mainstream: Meat and Poultry Raised without Routine Antibiotics Use" (2015, December 1). Retrieved January 5, 2016, from http://www.nrdc.org/food/files/antibiotic-free-meats-CS.pdf.

7 Michael Pollan (2010, May 20) "The Food Movement Rising." *New York Review of Books*, 10 June 2010. Retrieved 23 October 2015, from http://www.nybooks.com/articles/2010/06/10/food-movement-rising/.

8 "Nationwide Surveys Reveal Disconnect between Americans and Their Food" (2011, September 22). Retrieved January 5, 2016, from http://www.fooddialogues.com/press-release/antibiotics/nationwide-surveys-reveal-disconnect-between-americans-and-their-food.

9 M. Glassman (2015, October 1) "Hungry for Information: Polling Americans on Their Trust in the Food System." Retrieved October 20, 2015, from http://www.thechicagocouncil.org/publication/hungry-information-polling-americans-their-trust-food-system?utm_source=Informz&utm_medium=Email&utm_campaign=Council.

10 "USDA ERS – Food Prices and Spending" (n.d.). Retrieved December 10, 2015, from http://www.ers.usda.gov/data-products/ag-and-food-statistics-charting-the-essentials/food-prices-and-spending.aspx.

11 K. D. Brownell, R. M. Puhl, M. B. Schwartz, and L. Rudd (eds) (2005) *Weight Bias: Nature, Consequences, and Remedies*, New York: The Guilford Press.

12 T. Andreyeva, R. M. Puhl, and K. D. Brownell (2008) "Changes in Perceived Weight Discrimination among Americans: 1995–1996 through 2004–2006," *Obesity (Silver Spring)*, 16: 1129–1134.

13 M. V. Roehling (1999) "Weight-based Discrimination in Employment: Psychological and Legal Aspects," *Personnel Psychology*, 52: 969–1017.

14 *2012 Food & Health Survey: Consumer Attitudes toward Food Safety, Nutrition and Health* (2012, May 22) Retrieved January 5, 2016, from http://www.foodinsight.org/2012_Food_Health_Survey_Consumer_ Attitudes_toward_Food_Safety_Nutrition_and_Health.

15 Edward Leigh Gibson (2006) "Emotional Influences on Food Choice: Sensory, Physiological and Psychological Pathways," *Physiology & Behavior*, 89(1): 53–61.

16 Laura Canetti, Eytan Bachar, and Elliot M Berry (2002) "Food and Emotion," *Behavioural Processes*, 60(2): 157–164.

17 F. Norwood and J. Lusk (2011) *Compassion, by the Pound: The Economics of Farm Animal Welfare*, New York: Oxford University Press.

18 J. K. Lusk, J. Roosen, and A. Bieberstein (2014) "Consumer Acceptance of New Food Technologies: Causes and Roots of Controversies," *Annual Review of Resource Economics*, 6(1): 381–405.

19 Benedetto De Martino, Dharshan Kumaran, Ben Seymour, and Raymond J. Dolan (2006) "Frames, Biases, and Rational Decision-making in the Human Brain," *Science*, 313(5787): 684–687. [DOI:10.1126/science.1128356.]

20 J. Lusk, email interview, July 16, 2015.

FROM THE SOURCE

A consumer's perspective on …

FOOD AND HEALTH

Ambition, curiosity, and eagerness. Not qualities that pair well with fatigue, mental fog, and physical discomfort. Why didn't I think to ask my doctor sooner? But what was I going to say? Those are horribly vague and utterly useless descriptions to tell a doctor. Almost as useless as the two months I spent journaling my incredibly varied diet and eating habits to try to target the issue.

During and after college I got to a place where I had streamlined an efficient schedule for tackling the constant feeling of being rundown or not engaged. I read all of the health advice available and proactively pursued all of the recommendations. I made sure there was time in my schedule for eight hours of sleep and a one- to two-hour nap after work as needed. No time for extracurriculars. I had to make sure I felt well enough to be productive at work every day. I forced myself to spin class and loaded up on fruits and vegetables, all whole grains. No dairy.

What was left? Constantly reevaluating the process. None of the persistence or diligence worked. My energy always lagged and faded. It was difficult enough to fully understand the reality I was living in myself, let alone communicate it to others. Of course, I was turned away by doctors time and time again with no answer in sight. And so the dysphoria about the body I was given grew and dissatisfaction crept into many facets of my life.

I became obsessed with food. I questioned it and I questioned the food our system was supplying. What was affecting me? Was it the processed nature of what I was eating? A strange additive? Maybe dietary guidelines are wrong. Maybe that blog I read about dairy being unnatural for humans to consume had some merit. As things worsened, I became totally crazed by figuring out whatever was plaguing me. Food was the only thing I had control over anymore. I tried everything. It became an insanely emotional issue – the only thing I clung to. The worse I felt, the stronger my symptoms, the more focused I became on what I put in my body. My relationships suffered. I couldn't be present with others, or myself. Some days I felt enraged, other days I felt helpless. I became susceptible to any health pseudoscience that crossed my path. I didn't check to see if there was any truth behind it. So desperate for a cure, I went to every extreme.

Years later, I was finally diagnosed with celiac disease. After all that, it came down to something so simple. My body is incapable of digesting or breaking down gluten. All of the extra nutrients I wasn't absorbing would just hang out in my belly. For some time after that, I liked to tell myself that no one would fully comprehend what I overcame and continue to face. It would have to be my little secret. Yet what was so ironic about that approach is that a health struggle driven by diet is not a singular experience by any stretch of the imagination.

You see, my diagnosis isn't the point of the story. It's more than that. Our physical and mental health is imperative to live the lives we want. Some people, people who have never faced a severe health struggle, can't relate to the obsession one can feel about their food. I, on the other hand? I understand completely. When nothing seems to be working, when we are struggling against unknown and unseen demons – it is often food that is the one thing that we can control. United States agriculture, unfairly or not, gets pulled into our food and health conversations.

It hasn't been the traditional role of agriculture to contribute to these conversations. Yet the public, consumers like me, who are passionate about food and health – and really want to know – are important. Agricultural stakeholders could tap into our interest in the food and health system. They could show their compassion for how their products affect the consumers in the end. They could tell a story about how agriculture impacts public health for the positive – not the negative – and share the knowledge we do have about food and health. This compassion might go a long, long way in the dialogue with consumers – those far away from the fields of Iowa – lost in their own world of uncertainty and confusion.

So many Americans deal with a daily struggle to maintain good health by getting the proper nutrition. We are a nation that wants to be at our best. But it's not always within our control. We're limited by all kinds of circumstances, including our education about food, health, and our food system. Many of us, including a dear friend of mine, are still seeking a diagnosis. She has had to come to terms with the reality that food science and environmental science aren't advanced enough to give us all the right answers, right now. And while there is a lot of good science out there about agriculture and health, there could be more, and we could do a better job of sharing what already exists that *is* well researched and scientifically regarded.

For those in agriculture, I ask that you respect and understand those who desperately seek answers about their food. Their seeming "irrationality" is often driven by causes and symptoms that produce desperation, something you could sympathize with if you took the time. Don't despise us or look down on us, please. Understand us, and encourage the growth of a system that rewards quality communication on important food issues.

7

COMMUNICATING THE
ESSENCE OF AGRICULTURE

You can't just say, "Tell your story and write a blog." It's so
much more than that.

(Jolene Brown, author and farmer)

Agriculture today is trying to meet the rising tide of consumer
interest in their field. Some farms have opened their doors to the
public and farm bloggers are popping up to share their stories.
Agribusinesses are responding to inquiries to try to prevent false
accusations from spiraling out of control. College courses and degrees
are available for students interested in agricultural communications in
the modern world. Messages emphasize increased productivity and
efficiency, while voices remind consumers of agriculture's globally
focused intent to "feed the world."

Communicating effectively in the twenty-first century often
means finding that tricky balance between crafting a concise message
for people with little time to understand an entire industry, while
still meeting their desire to make good choices for themselves and
the world. As agriculture confronts the need to coordinate a
contemporary communications effort to the public, the challenges
can appear overwhelming. Like any new pursuit, there is a wealth

of concerns to consider: Who is responsible? What's the message? How do we coordinate it?

In this chapter, we look at the themes dominating how agriculture communicates with non-agricultural audiences, those being: agricultural messages haven't resonated – and often don't resonate – well, there are elements of agriculture that it is intrinsically difficult to communicate about, limited resources stunt many of agriculture's communication efforts. As we progress through these themes, we get into some of the finer points of communicating the essence of agriculture strategically and with purpose.

Current messages in agriculture focus on what agriculture *itself* must achieve for a growing population. While these messages resonate with farmers who are planning their business, they don't always resonate with audiences outside of agriculture. "Agriculture's standard 'go-to' messages aren't providing peace of mind for consumer audiences, and fighting emotion with science and facts has not moved the needle," writes Richard Cornett, communication professional, about research funded by the US Farmers & Ranchers Alliance. He explains disparity between what is said and what is heard. "Farmer [says] – Most farms are family run. Consumer hears – But beholden to big processors; Farmer – We keep food affordable. Consumer hears – But at what expense to quality? Farmer – We have the safest food supply in the world. Consumer hears – Pesticides, antibiotics and hormones may not be safe in the long run."[1]

Part of ensuring that a message resonates with an audience is making sure to select the *right* audience. Coordinating one all-encompassing message to capture all audiences is nigh on impossible. Targeting audiences who will actually hear and process messages means selecting the right people and providing the *relevant* information.[2] This information is likely to only be effective when it addresses specific information needs.[3] Much of the information already out there simply fails to meet consumers' needs.[4] Today, most associations and businesses within agriculture recognize the importance of targeting audiences – their ability to do so, however, is widely dependent on resources, a matter we delve into later in this chapter.

Information craved by a particular consumer can depend on demographics, socioeconomics, their attitudes, knowledge and preferences – and it can differ from our own personal preferences. We can't rely on our own personal experiences and norms to shape messaging.

Agriculture is a modern enterprise – and, put crassly, no one really gets that. The practice of modern farming is almost unrecognizable to consumers today. Agriculture has evolved and, rooted in visions of the past, people can cling to beliefs of what it *once was* to frame their understanding and approach towards it today. What we imagine farming 'should be' or 'has historically been' is, at its best, rural, romantic, and pastoral – although ironically farming has never lived up to our romantic expectations in its long history. Yet many cling to an outdated image of the 'ideal farm,' and with an old-fashioned idea of what the farm is, technology's encroachment onto the scene appears suspect.

The romanticism of farming was recognized by several of our interviewees. Journalists have covered the issue extensively. "Stop Romanticizing Farms," was published in 2014 in *Modern Farmer.* "Why it's Time to Stop Romanticizing Where Our Food Comes From," was in the *Guardian* in 2014. "Report Highlights Disconnect between Public Perception of Agriculture and Contemporary Ag Practices" was posted in 2014 by *Better Farming.* "Farming is Full of Shit, Blood, and Stubborn Fields. How's That for Romantic?" was published in *Grist* in 2014.

This may explain why so many messages haven't resonated, or don't resonate. Agriculture could instead relay the *value* of being a modern enterprise – and it could do so in a number of different ways. Communications expert Kevin Murphy explained, "Marketing is the art of communicating your essence; agriculture needs to lead with ethical and moral stories of what they do and why they do it." Today, United States agriculture provides things we take for granted or seldom think twice about. The modernity of agriculture and technological advances have played an absolutely critical role in getting us there. Painting this message with a broad brush doesn't work, though.

Agriculture provides a great deal of choice to a diverse set of consumer preferences and needs, just as messaging ought to. Brown said, "I wish that food shoppers knew that all types and sizes of agriculture are needed to feed our family and the world – local, organic, natural, CSA, farmers' markets, conventional and commercial. But we must be careful in the righteousness of a personal preference, because there is a need far beyond our singular choice."

There are some segments of consumers who, already heavily interested and invested in public health and sustainability, are interested in agricultural operations and how they can be improved. The Field to Market Alliance[5] is an initiative to bring together growers, agribusiness, companies, conservation groups, universities, and public-sector partners with a focus on measuring and advancing sustainability. It is an initiative that demonstrates, through data and actions, how agricultural interests can align with societal values. Communicating these specific initiatives can avoid the nitty-gritty of a farm operation while still directly relating to growing consumer interest and understanding. As Dr. Allan Gray said, "It's not a message of 'just trust us,' but a message that 'we are striving to learn and understand more and improve our operations every day.'" Agriculture strives to understand elements of public health and the impacts of farm operations on the environment and public health – but communicating about this is in its infancy.

There are pieces of agriculture that are intrinsically tough to communicate and that cloud messages and conversations. The 'business' element of farming and agriculture is one sticky point for the public. There is a misconception that the majority of farms in the United States are large corporations, when in fact most farms are family businesses. Farms that are owned and operated by family groups continue to dominate agricultural production in the United States, even as production has shifted to larger family businesses. Today, 96 percent of US farms with crop production are family farms.[6]

This doesn't change the reality that farming *is* a business. This is not understood well by the broader public, and is frequently perceived negatively. In many cases, though, the incentives to run a successful business often correlate with the incentive to maintain happy animals and healthy soil. This can translate into sustaining the soil for future use, recycling nutrients to keep costs down, and utilizing precision technologies to map the right amount of nitrogen to prevent over application and prevent waste of costly inputs. There has also been an evolution of conservation techniques that haven't gotten much media attention: cover crops that replenish nutrients, buffer zones to help to protect water quality, and lagoons of livestock waste that are recycled as nutrients for crop use. Farmers are likely to pass their farm down to a family member, an additional drive for them to be stewards of the land.

In addition, agriculture is by its very definition a practice that 'cultivates land.' It's an industry that has to use the land to feed people, and that sometimes means taking something from the earth, such as water and nutrients. This is a difficult concept for the public to grasp. Each of us, as an individual, drives the use of this land to sustain our life. Most of our fresh water, for instance, is used for agriculture.[7] [8] It can be a bit grim to have to try and communicate the message that your industry, by its very nature, *must* use the land's precious resources, even if it is trying to do so responsibly. This misunderstanding of the fundamental truth of agriculture often muddies the fact that much of agriculture is trying, all the time, to produce more with fewer and fewer resources because the amount of the world's arable land is limited – and our population is growing.

Framing a message that resonates and understanding the unique difficulties in communicating a topic are important – but so is another element: resources. This is an important concern for agriculture. John Stika, President of Certified Angus Beef® brand, was one of many interviewees to make this point about agriculture at large: "We have 2 percent of the population trying to communicate to 98 percent. It's a function of resources. And the challenge is knowing where the resources come from to make sure the information is being factually shared." Not only does agriculture need to update their messages, but they often need to go back and correct where communication went wrong – or where it was absent and misinformation fomented. "It's harder to extract information and insert the facts than it is to take an empty slot and insert the facts," he explained.

The structure of farming itself is not conducive to easily organized, cohesive communication efforts. Farmers are working solo or only with a few family members or employees. There is no communications or public relations department helping them to craft their image or maintain positive relations with consumers at large. Farmers' experiences and perspectives are vastly different from those of consumers who grew up far away from the realities and frustrations of weather and climate.

Most farmers don't have the resources for formal communication and it is unreasonable to expect them to rely on their personal incentive. Farming, for instance, can be very individual in nature. "It's probably not fair to paint farmers with such a broad brush," Dr. Michael Gunderson, Professor at the Center for Food and Agribusiness, told us, "But I would say most of them are fairly introverted people. They're not engaged in a profession where a lot of them get out and interact with the public, or even their own customers. That makes it hard. You have a group of people that are very passionate about what they do, and they do it very well, but many are not really interested in talking about it." Gunderson wasn't the only interviewee to mention this in an interview. Don Villwock, President of the Indiana Farm Bureau, stated that, "Farmers are for the most part an introverted and a very humble sector of our society. For them to go public, to expose themselves to public scrutiny, makes them very uncomfortable."

Anecdotal evidence does not make a scientific case for a generalized farmer 'character,' but considering the nature of a farmer's work – and how this impacts their outreach with society – is worthwhile. Farmers generally work alone or with only a couple of other people. The job requires focus and hard work, which is for the most part solitary work. Being a successful farmer requires many skills, but communications was never traditionally an essential requirement. You can't talk a potato into existence, but you *can* ensure that the soil composition is ideal for that particular crop. The very nature of farming simply makes it difficult or impossible to have a strong, unified collection of resources for communication.

Farmers most certainly have important ideas to contribute, but they are simply not equipped to shoulder the sole responsibility of explaining agriculture. It requires extreme effort and hard work to understand all aspects of such a complex system – the human health impact, ethical conversations, environmental impacts, to name just a few. Moreover, to contextualize this into the larger economic picture is simply not a function farmers can fill. Academics and researchers are uniquely positioned to contribute, although lacking in incentives – a critical issue we address in Chapter 10.

Despite the challenges of a full-time job and massive time constraints, communications can become a hobby for the highly motivated and outgoing farmer. There are indeed farmers who are making an impressive effort to communicate. For the Love of Beef, The Real Farmwives of America, the Peterson Brothers and many more are trying to answer questions about what they do and why they do it, or share a more accurate presentation of who they are. The Peterson Brothers are veritable celebrities in the agricultural world. These three strapping, handsome young lads, with charming smiles and sleeveless t-shirts, have a YouTube page where their parodies of pop songs reworked with agriculture-based lyrics count their views in the tens of millions.[9] "Farmer Style" (a parody of "Gangnam Style") has 16 million views.[10] These homegrown videos are only part of their efforts. They give talks, have an active blog, and host tours on their farm during the summers.

"We're trying to tell the truth," Greg Peterson, eldest of the brothers, told us. "We want farming to be represented accurately. We want farmers to be pictured accurately. That's definitely not true in movies and TV shows and on the internet. People either have this romantic old-time view of farmers where they are wearing overalls and carrying around a pitchfork, or they have this new misrepresented idea of farmers where they are big corporations or big industrial-type farms. Neither of those are correct."[11] Although it's unclear whether the Peterson Brothers are having the impact they hope for, their motives are spot on.

Membership associations are a major resource available to farmers and the agricultural community. Farmers pay dues and the association can collectively represent them. Many of the associations are centered toward a particular commodity. The Corn Growers Association has a focus on corn, the Cotton Association has a focus on cotton, etc. These associations have not, in the past, been geared towards communicating with the public, but instead have been the voice of farmers in Washington (a voice that is also important as policymakers are ever-further from agriculture as well). Today, many associations have reoriented some of their resources to deliver a more positive message about agriculture – but these resources are limited. Chuck Conner, former United States Deputy Secretary of Agriculture and current President and CEO of the National Council of Farmer Cooperatives, said, "Moving the needle of American public opinion today is expensive and so farmers' willingness to fund those kinds of things is pretty limited. They [farmers] let us do some of it, but everything that we do is kind of on a shoestring budget."

The resources to fund broader campaigns to communicate positive messages and target concerns are limited in many areas of agriculture. Association funding is often found to be better spent promoting a product to companies that use and process commodities supplied by agriculture. This *directly* benefits farmers. In turn, food companies shoulder the task of communicating with consumers through marketing their particular product, because this directly benefits them. These companies have a stake in promoting their product, but not necessarily agriculture as a whole.

A lack of coordination and resources creates lost opportunities. An interviewee provided the example of a cobranded press release between the Humane Society and Dunkin' Donuts. The release delivered the news that Dunkin' Donuts was committed to sourcing 100 percent cage-free eggs by 2015.[12] This announcement was featured on *CNBC*, in the *Wall Street Journal*, the *Huffington Post*, the *Boston Globe*, the *Chicago Tribune*, Fortune.com, *Business Insider*, Consumerist.com, and more. They didn't instigate the agreement or get on the news release – but those working in agriculture, inevitably, will be the ones to deliver on the promise. Yet the Humane Society gets the air time, the quotations, the credit, the name recognition, the applause. Our interviewee called this a travesty for agriculture – and one that should be a 'wake-up call.' Agriculture should be seeking the partnerships, putting out the releases, leveraging resources, and seeking opportunities.

Setting goals, concentrating finite resources, and identifying audiences can make this possible. Goal-setting in communications can be difficult because of the intangible nature of the results. In most cases, it's hard to clearly pinpoint the benefits and impacts, particularly in the environment of a non-profit association that relies on members seeing value in its services. There needs to be a collective reckoning, however, and that's been happening in many corners. Conner told us quite frankly, "I'm still not to the point where I would say that we're doing it well. Maybe we're not doing it terribly, like we were ten years ago, but we're not doing it well."

The essence of our modern agricultural system is not glamorous. It never was, and likely never will be. It is charged with taking care of some of the basic things that we, in the developed world, are almost all lucky enough to be able to take for granted. And although not glamorous, it is a system that is effective at meeting diverse needs. It's efficient and productive. New practices are making it more environmentally sound.

Feeding a growing world is absolutely one of the most important things our agricultural system does (in accordance with most people's moral and ethical beliefs). Yet in many areas, regions, and swaths of the population, people's concerns have moved beyond this. Getting at the essence of agriculture means moving deeper than this, getting into the particulars of certain issues, and connecting with the public through a more collaborative conversation.

Notes

1 R. Cornett (2011, November 1) "Agriculture's Message Not Resonating with the Public." Retrieved February 10, 2016, from http://westernfarmpress.com/government/agriculture-s-message-not-resonating-public?page=1.

2 W. Verbeke (2005) "Agriculture and the Food Industry in the Information Age," *European Review of Agricultural Economics*, 32(3): 347–368.

3 A. M. Rubin (1986) "Uses, Gratifications and Media Effects Research," in J. Bryant and D. Zillmann (eds.), *Perspectives in Media Effects*, Hillsdale, NJ: Lawrence Erlbaum, pp. 281–301.

4 Y. Salaün and K. Flores (2001) "Information Quality: Meeting the Needs of the Consumer," *International Journal of Information Management*, 21(1): 21–37.

5 "About Us" (n.d.). Retrieved February 10, 2016, from https://www.fieldtomarket.org/about-us/.

6 "Farm Size and the Organization of U.S. Crop Farming" (2013, August 1). Retrieved October 24, 2015, from http://www.ers.usda.gov/media/1156726/err152.pdf.

7 M. Falkenmark and G. Lindh (1993) "Water and Economic Development," in P. H. Gleick (ed.), *Water in Crisis: A Guide to the World's Fresh Water Resources*, New York: Oxford University Press, pp. 80–91.

8 D. Pimentel, J. Houser, E. Preiss, O. White, H. Fang, L. Mesnick, T. Barsky, S. Tariche, J. Schreck, and S. Alpert (1997) "Water Resources: Agriculture, the Environment, and Society," *BioScience*, 47(2): 97–106.

9 "Peterson Farm Bros." *YouTube*. YouTube. Web. 12 August 2015, https://www.youtube.com/user/ThePetersonFarmBros.

10 "Farmer Style (Gangnam Style Parody)." *YouTube*. YouTube. Web. 12 August 2015, https://www.youtube.com/watch?v=LX153eYcVrY.

11 Greg Peterson, email interview, July 2015.

12 "Dunkin' Donuts, with The Humane Society of the United States, Announces Timeline for Sourcing 100 Percent Cage-Free Eggs" (2015, December 7). Retrieved February 3, 2016, from http://www.prnewswire.com/news-releases/dunkin-donuts-with-the-humane-society-of-the-united-states-announces-timeline-for-sourcing-100-percent-cage-free-eggs-300188410.html.

A rancher's perspective on ...

BLOGGING AND OUTREACH

Debbie Lyons-Blythe began blogging in 2009 to share the realities of life on the ranch. Her goal is to fill in the blanks for people who are unfamiliar with rural life and to connect with her non-agricultural readership. Here she answers questions on how and why she prioritizes communication and outreach.

Why did you start blogging?

In the summer of 2009, a close relative's daughter who is one generation removed from the farm visited our farm to get away from her city life in Denver and to experience the environment where her mother was raised in White City, Kansas. Since then, this relative has been bringing her young family to the farm every summer. They fish in the farm ponds, feed the show heifers, drive ATVs, and ride in the tractors with my kids. While they were here, she demonstrated concern about the safety of beef – particularly antibiotic residue and hormones in milk. It became clear to me that despite her heritage, she was not raised on the farm and does not understand these issues the way we do. And she is just one generation removed from agricultural life! How can we expect those who are two or three generations removed to be able to understand these issues? We in agriculture are doing a terrible job of explaining why and what we do. When she and her family left after that first trip, I started my blog and had two posts written by the time they reached home from their eight-hour drive.

What are you trying to achieve?

The original goal of my blog was to "tell our story" and provide a glimpse of what happens on a Kansas cattle ranch. As the years went on, my blog evolved to not only "tell" but to also ask questions of my own and to "connect" and have "conversations" with my readers. I am focused on people who don't work in production agriculture – so if I get one comment, share, or tweet from a non-ag person for each blog post I write, I consider that a success. I write posts about specific activities on the ranch and explain what and why we do things. I even share personal stories like my son's health challenges, things that have nothing to do with ranching but everything to do with being a mom.

My goal is also to show that I am a regular person and a consumer too. I have the same concerns. There are so many times that we put ourselves on opposite sides of the fence in discussions with consumers. My job requires work boots and leather gloves, while other moms put on pumps and dress clothes – but we are both working to feed our family, keep our home, do our jobs, and give our kids the best. We are not producers vs. consumers ... we are all consumers. I look for ways to show our similarities, instead of our differences.

What topics really confuse the general public about your farm operations?

Sustainability is a tough subject. It means so many different things to different people. I am a founding member of the US Roundtable for Sustainable Beef (USRSB) and they define sustainability as "a socially responsible, environmentally sound and economically viable product that prioritizes Planet; People; Animals and Progress." However, I think that my grandpa defined it even more clearly: "Leave the land better than when you found it."

Farmers and ranchers often become defensive when the topic of sustainability comes up because, seriously, who is more sustainable than a fifth-generation cattle rancher? Yet we need to engage in discussions about sustainability so that we can demonstrate how we have been maintaining and improving the environment for hundreds of years. I recently told my New Jersey cousin about my involvement in the USRSB. I was so excited to share it with him and thought he would appreciate what we are doing. His response was, "It is about time! We've been talking about sustainability for ages! Finally you farmers are starting to think about it. There are so many ways you need to improve."

I was shocked and predictably I became defensive. However, I didn't immediately respond. We were at supper together so I took a deep breath, sipped my water, and thought about what he had said. He is the perfect example of a highly educated, morally focused consumer. He truly believed that someone outside of agriculture had "invented" sustainability. I realized he is exactly the type of person concerned about sustainability who needs a farmer/rancher perspective. We are on the same page, but he doesn't realize it. Usually the farmer/rancher gets fired up when a consumer has this response (as I initially did), but we need to take the opportunity to communicate. Although we haven't labeled it with a fancy term, we have been working on sustainability for generations. Farmers and ranchers were focused on passing their land on to the next generation long before the term "sustainable" became a buzzword.

What strategies do you employ when writing and promoting your blog? What could be helpful for others who wish to communicate agriculture?

It can feel difficult to share our story. Yet it's helpful to the majority of consumers who only hear negative things about agriculture from the small percentage of people who are very loudly opposed to it. Most people just want to make good decisions, buy good food, and do the best for their families. Predictably, they have an ear to social media and have heard rumors. Naturally, they have questions. I welcome those kind of people to come and actually ask.

I am clear that I am not selling "Debbie's beef." I do not market my own meat. I carefully point out that I am a typical cattle rancher in Kansas. Every region raises their cattle differently, but in my area nearly every rancher has the same basic concerns and responsibilities. Therefore I ensure that I am clearly and appropriately communicating what happens on my ranch and that I am no one special. If someone reads my blog and thinks, "I want to find her beef – not the regular meat in the store," then I have failed. My goal is to communicate that the beef in the grocery store and restaurant is raised by people *like* me. It is all safe and nutritious and the ranchers do their best by the animals with sustainability always in mind.

What should communicators 'on both sides of the fence' know?

If I want to know what goes on inside a steel mill, who should I ask? Would the activist demonstrating against the mill's emissions be an unbiased source of information? Would the owner of the mill be open and honest? If I really want to know what happens on the working floor of a steel mill, I should ask my uncle who works there. On the same note, if someone wants to know what happens on a farm or ranch, they should ask someone who drives a tractor, vaccinates calves, feeds hay during snowstorms, works 80+ hour weeks year-round, and raises their kids doing the same thing their grandparents did. Go to the source. Ask a farmer or rancher.

To the agricultural community? We have to be open to those questions and available for discussions – whether online or face to face. One of my favorite places to advocate about beef is in the grocery store when I'm heading out to shop. I don't need to buy beef as I have a freezer full of it. However, I always swing by the meat case and watch what people are doing. I nearly always engage someone in conversation as they select beef. How are you going to cook that? What are you planning for supper? Have you ever tried a flatiron steak? If I can get a little conversation going, I tell them that I am a rancher and I love to talk to people about beef. They almost always ask a question back. It's just a quick minute or two of conversation but if I can make one person think of me when they pick up a package or two of beef and feel good about it … then I count that as a success.

8

THE IMPORTANCE OF PERCEPTION

A couple of years ago I worked a booth at a dietetics conference. We fielded questions about GMOs and heritage seeds and handed out papaya samples. But more than once, I had people come up to the booth and ask, "So what does Monsanto do? I have heard they are evil, but I really have no idea why people say that." ... pause ... perfect example of the majority of people who just want to make good decisions, buy good food, and do the best for their families, but they do have an ear to social media and have heard rumors.

(Debbie Lyons-Blythe, farm blogger)

In Chapter 1, we saw that the 'grossness' of 'pink slime' was perceived to be a health threat when in fact lean textured beef is safe for consumption. In Chapter 2, we looked at how Chipotle is shaping consumer perception in order to portray their company in a better light. In Chapter 3, we saw how a blogger's or celebrity's perception of 'truth' can be warped by attitude or motivation. In Chapter 5, we saw how the public's perception of the health risks of GMOs don't align with reality.

There is an abundance of literature in academia that focuses exclusively on perception and communication. Articles, books, and courses dig deeply into the relationship between these two. Even for those who aren't communication scholars, it is likely most have already heard the age-old marketing adage that 'perception is reality,' upon which, the very next day, you might hear the conflicting comment from an irritated loved one, "Your perception isn't reality!"

"Our conscious perception of the world, though relatively stable, is not static. We are incapable of being fully objective, even in our most mundane observations and impressions. Our awareness of the objects around us is informed and fine-tuned by any number of transient factors – our strength and energy levels, our sense of confidence, our fears and desires. Being human means seeing the world through your own, constantly shifting, lens," writes Dr. Christof Koch of the California Institute of Technology in *Scientific American.*

Perception and its role in communication are multifaceted and can be examined from a number of different angles. At its core, perception is the process of how we select, organize, and interpret our sensory information. We communicate on the basis of our perceptions, which do not necessarily align with each other's.[1] Perception matters because it becomes each individual's personal reality. It dictates how we receive future communications, and above all it dictates behavior.

In this chapter, we home in on the role of perception in the context of communication in food and agriculture as it directly relates to our dialogue today. When there is an information void, or rampant misinformation, negative or positive perceptions of topics, companies, organizations, and risk can easily blur together and overlap – even when they are separate matters and don't warrant standing under the same umbrella. To add to this, when exposed to the same information or message, different people respond differently based on their personalities, values, involvement, education, and more.

Risk is an extremely important element of perception in food and agriculture. The public's appetite for risk, and their perception of risk, can largely define how they respond. It surfaces frequently, swaying the dialogue and flavoring the receptiveness of the public. We saw this misalignment when we took an in-depth look at the case of GMOs. Overwhelming research points to the conclusion that GMOs are safe, yet there has been a backlash against it in public opinion. To dig deeper into the nuances, one of the particulars people question is GMOs and their weed resistance. Many genetically modified crops have been designed to tolerate glyphosate, the active ingredient in Roundup. Tolerance to glyphosate is what allows farmers to spray GM crops and kill the weeds but not the corn or soy. The United States Environmental Protection Agency (EPA) reports that due to the low dosages it presents very little threat of toxicity to humans. It is slightly toxic to birds and practically nontoxic to fish, aquatic invertebrates, and honeybees.[2]

A well-researched article in the the *Washington Post* strives, in a laudable attempt, to shed light on this exact issue in a balanced manner. The headline, however – "It's the Chemical Monsanto Depends On. How Dangerous Is It?" – raises a bigger issue about public perception and agricultural businesses that we explore later in the chapter. For now, though, we will stay focused on glyphosate. Not only does journalist Tamar Haspel write about the extremely low doses of glyphosate that could ever find their way into our food, but she also writes: "One definite positive here is that herbicide tolerance has enabled farmers to reduce tillage, traditionally used to uproot and kill weeds. Because tilling disturbs the soil, it facilitates erosion and runoff of nutrients and chemicals. Reduce tilling, and you reduce those problems and retain more water in the bargain."[3]

Technologies associated with GMOs are not alone in suffering from the misalignment of public perception of risk. Another example is public concern over the impact of hormone use in dairy cattle on human health and development. In a nutshell, bovine somatotropin (bST) is a naturally occurring growth hormone in lactating dairy cows, and rbST is a synthetic version of this hormone that is used in dairy cattle to increase milk production by 10–15 percent. There has been intense speculation among the public that it is bad for human health and induces onset of puberty for young girls. This is despite numerous studies showing that no threat has been found. It has been approved by the FDA. If any risk is present, it is extremely low.[4,5] An article in the peer reviewed *Journal of Diary Science* explained that "More than 1000 bST studies have been conducted, which involved over 20,000 dairy cows, and results have been confirmed by scientists throughout the world. This quantity of published research is unprecedented for a new technology and greater than most dairy technologies in use."[6]

A safety assessment conducted by researchers found that "Scientific evidence shows there is no change in the composition of milk from cows supplemented with rbST, and therefore no changes are present in the milk and dairy products from rbST-supplemented cows that could affect the age at puberty."[7] They go on to discuss that the environmental factors actually responsible are the increasing weight and height of boys and girls over the past century. Chronic conditions, nutritional status, and weight gain are important determinants of the onset of puberty – not rbST.

These two examples – glyphosate and rbST – are just two cases amongst many of misdirected concern due to misaligned perceptions of risk. There *are* potential areas of concern, it is disingenuous to pretend otherwise – for instance weed resistance to glyphosate, increased risk of mastitis (a common inflammatory reaction of the udder tissue in dairy cows when they produce a lot of milk), and the resulting increase of antibiotic use – but when focus is on the wrong issues, they consume all the proverbial airtime and other more important areas are neglected.

"Advances in social and decision sciences have enhanced the understanding of lay risk perceptions and the development of risk communications," write Senior Advisor in Global Food Policy, US Department of State, Jack Bobo and Associate Director of the Institute on Science for Global Policy, Sweta Chakraborty. "Taking into account how the public perceives and assesses risks are integral for communication plans. Specifically, consideration of public trust as a factor in the shaping of risk perceptions is required for effective risk communication."[8]

As Bobo and Chakraborty explained, if the public is suspicious or untrusting of a source, it will shape their perception of risk. So if an entity, or person, is not trusted by the public, it's important to take this into account when communicating and developing a plan – because it will shape how the messages are received. It does matter who delivers the message. The public often perceive themselves to be out of control in decision-making relating to new agricultural technologies. Regulators and scientists should be cognizant of this.[9]

We will now take a look at one case where the notoriety of a large company permeates other elements of the conversation. Monsanto is an agricultural business, or as they are commonly known within the industry, an agribusiness. Agribusiness, a word marriage between 'agriculture' and 'business,' was coined sometime in the last century. It refers to the range of activities and disciplines encompassed by modern food production. This can run the gamut from agrichemicals, breeding, crop production, farm machinery, processing, seed supply to marketing and retail sales. Agribusinesses have grown in size in the last few decades and this only subjects them to more criticism and skepticism.

Modern Farmer recently published the article "Why Does Everyone Hate Monsanto?" "In recent years, no company has been more associated with evil than Monsanto. But why?" writes journalist Lessley Anderson.[10] In a basic Google search for the name 'Monsanto,' the fourth website to pop up is *Millions Against Monsanto*, the fifth is an article called "Monsanto's Harvest of Fear," the sixth is *March Against Monsanto – It's Time to Take Our Planet Back*. The list goes on. *Vanity Fair* published an article condemning them ruthlessly. "Monsanto already dominates America's food chain with its genetically modified seeds. Now it has targeted milk production. Just as frightening as the corporation's tactics – ruthless legal battles against small farmers – is its decades-long history of toxic contamination."[11]

Many still associate Monsanto with Agent Orange. Agent Orange was one of 15 herbicides used by the US military as a defoliant in the Vietnam War. It was later revealed to cause serious health issues – including tumors, birth defects, rashes, psychological symptoms, and cancer – among returning US servicemen and their families as well as among the Vietnamese population. A painful legacy for a painful war during a painful time in our country. From 1965 to

1969, Monsanto Company was one of nine wartime government contractors which manufactured Agent Orange. The government set the specifications for making Agent Orange and determined when, where, and how it was used. Culpability and guilt are still heatedly discussed in different circles.

March Against Monsanto is an activist group that is, as its name would denote, quite outspoken against the company. Its website, www.MarchAgainstMonsanto.com, prominently displays a tab titled 'AGENT ORANGE.' The page associated with that tab states:

> We want the world to know that the company trying to dominate the global food supply, and telling you that GMOs are safe to eat, are nothing more than murderers who should be tried and convicted. Monsanto, will tell you that they were contracted by the United States Government and therefore should have no accountability for the travesties created by Agent Orange. In fact, as the largest producer of Agent Orange, Monsanto themselves knew that the chemical was deadly. Besides, even in the worst case scenario, it doesn't take a genius to figure out that there might be serious danger to humans if they are coming into contact with a chemical that turned lush green jungles into barren wastelands in a matter of hours.[12]

Somehow, amidst all the emotion and indignation of a painful historical memory, the author of this piece managed to slide GMOs into a conversation that *is not* about GMOs (similar to what we saw earlier in the case of the *Washington Post* headline). In this particular example, his/her point is to discuss reparations to the victims of Agent Orange. Yet now, GMOs are linked to Agent Orange and to "murderers who should be tried and convicted," in a piece written by an unknown author on a blog. This is not an obscure blog with a small readership. The March Against Monsanto Facebook page has almost one million likes.[13]

The question "Is the misuse of a herbicide during wartime the fault of the company who produced it or the fault of the government who ordered its production and then ordered its use?" has no relevance to a contemporary debate on GMOs. It is an important question, but is unrelated to genetically modified organisms. Monsanto didn't invent GMOs. Academics did.[14] Companies such as Monsanto hold patents to particular GMOs, but they didn't invent the concept.

How do these illogical leaps happen? How do unrelated topics get lumped under a negative umbrella of distrust and fear? Perception. People rely on their perception of agriculture to filter the information that they receive about agricultural issues. If a person's knowledge of Monsanto is limited to a vague association with alleged war crimes, and then they hear that Monsanto produces GMOs, they process this information based on their limited knowledge (in addition to personality, culture, etc.). Effective communication, when understood in this light, is significantly more challenging and nuanced. It requires a deep understanding of the 'other,' or the audience. For instance, the Non-GMO Project held a Non-GMO Facebook challenge. One of the winners was a mom who submitted a photo of her smiling baby lying next to a piece of paper stating, "My mom won't eat GMOs so I don't have to drink them!"[15] Over one million people follow the Non-GMO Project on Facebook. Different viewers of this photo can perceive it dramatically differently. A young mom who works in finance, with no agricultural background, may become worried and concerned about the health of her child. She could become paranoid that, because of her inattention to food issues, she may be slowly poisoning her infant through her breast milk. A farmer, on the other hand, may scoff at the 'ignorance' of consumers and shrug it off as silliness.

The perception of Monsanto as an untrusted corporation has a powerful, detrimental effect not just on them, but on many other issues that confront agriculture today. Monsanto is perceived poorly by a very vocal swath of the population, and this becomes the filter through which many people receive any and all communications about agriculture. Monsanto has made a large effort in the last couple of years to engage in a productive dialogue with consumers. They are fighting a tough battle.

Monsanto started to make communication a priority in late 2013, early 2014. Global Corporate Engagement Lead of Monsanto,

Jesus Madrazo, stated in an interview with us in early 2015, "We [Monsanto] have underestimated the growing needs of consumers. They want to learn more about where their food comes from, how it's produced … We realized that we needed to do more and we needed to take our voice out of agriculture and to the consumers. That's what we have been doing, especially in the last 18 months or so."

Politico published an article in late 2013 called "Monsanto's Makeover." "The ostrich approach to public relations has not yielded dividends for the company's image," writes journalist Jenny Hopkinson. "In recent months the company has shaken up its senior public relations staff, upped its relationship with one of the nation's largest public relations firms and helped launch a website designed to combat the fallacies surrounding genetically modified organisms."

One of their new initiatives is a website, Discover Monsanto, with the slogan 'Be part of the conversation.'[16] Anyone can submit a question and they publicly post their responses. According to Madrazo, Monsanto is now trying to actively listen to what consumers want and directly engage with them. We tested it, and a response was posted within the week.

JESSICA AND WHITNEY: When bloggers say things that are not scientifically proven, how do you try to combat that kind of misinformation?

MONSANTO: Hi Jessica and Whitney. While more people, including bloggers, are joining the conversation about food in our country and around the world, we realize the need to join this dialogue and make the correct information available. We want to participate in these important discussions and be transparent about who we are and what we do. That's why we created The Conversation on our Discover site – to have a conversation and answer people's questions. We hope it's a two-way dialogue and that people will be just as open to hearing from us as we are to hearing from them.

This was an innocuous question, yet they aren't only responding to easy pitches. Some of the tough ones are:

KOLY M: Why are you suing Vermont?

MICHELLE M: If you can sue a small farmer for GMO's accidentally getting in their crop, can I sue you if they are found in my organic child's body?

JESSIKA W: If you have nothing to hide, why do you continue to spend millions of dollars to prevent GMO labeling?

This kind of website, and interactive communication, is very new to Monsanto. "This is how agribusiness is different now than it was a couple of years ago. Any company or stakeholder that is concerned with agriculture, communication is a key thing we have to do," Madrazo said.

Monsanto, and other agribusinesses, are starting to change their approach. One of the ways Monsanto claims to be doing this is by listening to what consumers want. "We start from the very basics, quite frankly. We started to go to those forums and just listen and understand, instead of trying to drive our own messages," said Madrazo. "They want to learn more about where their food comes from, how it's produced, and the role of farmers in companies like Monsanto in that process."

Monsanto, like many other pieces and parts of agriculture, is playing a tough game of catch-up. Consumer interest in agriculture has been growing for decades. Agriculture's communication efforts, however, have really only trended upwards recently. For many years, while consumer interest grew, agricultural players were not actively shaping evolving perceptions by communicating on important issues. Now, people in agriculture are trying to meet consumer concerns but they have to find new ways to communicate about what they do.

While there will always be extremists on either end of the spectrum, for a long time extremist voices were the only ones being heard. This damaged not only the reputation of agriculture and agribusiness, but, as we saw, also debates on issues themselves. This shortage of balance and context, or general lack of communication, makes it a lose/lose situation for all the players.

Perception does not always align with fact. It does not intrinsically gravitate towards an objective, factual reality just because that objective, factual reality exists. According to research from The

Center for Food Integrity, being right is not enough to ensure your information is considered in the social decision-making process. Acceptance of innovations in agriculture will impact the well-being of farmers and consumers in the coming decades. Science and risk communication is a key determinant of the extent to which new technologies in food and agriculture will be accepted.[17] Concise messaging from a trusted source can help to aid the process. Communication needs to be crafted with an understanding of the receiver's perspective, and to do that the communicator may need to understand how to better combat the perceptions. This means listening to the concerns of important stakeholders and understanding their values so you can meet them where they are.[18] By listening carefully, organizations and people can start to understand what their audience's perceptions are and why they are that way.

Notes

1 S. Lane (2010) "Basics of Competent Communication," in *Interpersonal Communication: Competence and Contexts*, 2nd edition, Boston: Pearson, p. 4.

2 "Glyphosate" (2015, October 14). Retrieved February 9, 2016, from http://www.epa.gov/ingredients-used-pesticide-products/glyphosate.

3 T. Haspel (2015, October 4) "It's the Chemical Monsanto Depends On. How Dangerous Is It?" Retrieved February 10, 2016, from https://www.washingtonpost.com/lifestyle/food/its-the-chemical-monsanto-depends-on-how-dangerous-is-it/2015/10/04/2b8f58ee-67a0-11e5-9ef3-fde182507eac_story.html.

4 J. C. Juskevidi and C. G. Guyer (1990) "Bovine Growth Hormone: Human Food Safety Evaluation," *Science*, 249: 4971.

5 D. Grobe and R. Douthitt (1995) "Consumer Acceptance of Recombinant Bovine Growth Hormone: Interplay between Beliefs and Perceived Risks," *Journal of Consumer Affairs*, 29(1): 128–143.

6 D. E. Bauman (1992) "Bovine Somatotropin: Review of an Emerging Animal Technology," *Journal of Dairy Science*, 75(12): 3432–3451.

7 R. Raymond, C. W. Bales, R. D. E. Bauman, D. Clemmons, R. Kleinman, D. Lanna, … and K. Sejrsen (2009, July) "Recombinant Bovine Somatotropin (rbST): A Safety Assessment," in *Joint Annual Meeting of the American Dairy Science Association, Canadian Society of Animal Science, and American Society of Animal Science, Montreal, Canada*.

8 Jack Bobo (2015) "Pink Slime, Raw Milk and the Tweetification of Risk," *European Journal of Risk Regulation*, 6(1): 141–145.

9   L. Frewer, J. Lassen, B. Kettlitz, J. Scholderer, V. Beekman, and K. G. Berdal (2004) "Societal Aspects of Genetically Modified Foods," *Food and Chemical Toxicology*, 42(7): 1181–1193.

10 L. Anderson (2014, March 4) "Why Does Everyone Hate Monsanto?" *Modern Farmer*. Retrieved October 29, 2015, from http://modernfarmer. com/2014/03/monsantos-good-bad-pr-problem/.

11 D. Barlett and J. Steele (2008, May 1) "Monsanto's Cruel, and Dangerous, Monopolization on American Farming." Retrieved October 29, 2015, from http://www.vanityfair.com/news/2008/05/ monsanto200805.

12 "AGENT ORANGE" (n.d.). Retrieved October 30, 2015, from http://www.march-against-monsanto.com/agent-orange/.

13 March Against Monsanto (n.d.). Retrieved May 5, 2016, from https:// www.facebook.com/MarchAgainstMonsanto.

14 "Paul Berg, Herbert W. Boyer, and Stanley N. Cohen" (n.d.). Chemical Heritage Foundation. Retrieved January 4, 2016, from http://www. chemheritage.org/discover/online-resources/chemistry-in-history/ themes/pharmaceuticals/preserving-health-with-biotechnology/berg- boyer-cohen.aspx.

15 Facebook (n.d.). Retrieved October 30, 2015, from https://www. facebook.com/MarchAgainstMonsanto/.

16 (n.d.). Retrieved October 30, 2015, from http://discover.monsanto. com/.

17 J. L. Lusk, J. Roosen, and A. Bieberstein (2014) "Consumer Acceptance of New Food Technologies: Causes and Roots of Controversies," *Annual Review of Resource Economics*, 6(1): 381–405.

18 "Cracking the Code on Food Issues: Insights from Moms, Millenials and Foodies" (n.d.). *Consumer Trust Research, 2014*. Retrieved from http://www.foodintegrity.org/.

A policymaker's perspective on ...

IMPROVING COMMUNICATION WITH A CULTURAL REORIENTATION

Jim Moseley served as the Deputy Secretary of the US Department of Agriculture (USDA) from 2001 to 2005 and is currently a Co-Chair at AGree. He has played a vital role in developing public policy regarding agriculture, the environment, and natural resources conservation at the state and national levels. Here he answers questions on how we can enhance communication around food and agriculture.

From a farming and policymaker perspective, how can we improve communication in agriculture?

There is a tendency from agriculture to only present the affirmative in our occupation as farmers. This is natural and to be expected, and we should present the positive things that happen in our operations! However, this approach can also ignore or cover up some of the errors and mistakes that occur on the farm level. People eventually see through this deception and, when that happens, we lose credibility. When these matters aren't discussed and addressed, it also offers the opportunity for those who seek to diminish our standing with the public – such as those working for groups with sharply different views about how farming should be conducted – to do so. I would especially highlight activists who work in federal policy and have an ongoing interest in changing agriculture in ways that we, as farmers, would view as negative to our interests.

We certainly need to portray ourselves in a good light, but we need to also be honest and recognize that there are some areas that need improvement. If farm leaders, at any level, ignore significant public problems brought on by our farming population, they quickly lose the ability to engage credibly in the public debate (especially with the larger voting public, where there remains a significant voting advantage when public support is needed on farm issues in state and federal legislative processes).

What happens when things that need to be improved in agriculture get swept under the rug?

If we don't tell the entire truth about our farming practices and the potential impact on the lives of the non-farming public, that destines us for eventual difficulty in policy. Instead of being able to solve the problem using our historical structures – research, extension, and the legislative process (where we do have a voice) – we can quickly find ourselves being drawn into the court system in legal challenges. This places us before a single individual, a judge, whose responsibility is to make a definitive decision.

Decisions in court are not vetted and debated publicly as those in the legislative process are. This can result in defendants being dramatically harmed. Unfortunately, I have observed this situation and watched people spend their life savings attempting to defend themselves – not to mention the emotional toll it takes on a family when so affected. With planning and preparation at the farm level and by the industry's leadership, this can often be avoided.

It is relatively simple for those who are not directly involved in the agricultural production process to deliver easy answers. However, their solutions will seldom be viable, for a variety of reasons, not the least of which is simple practicality and/or the cost of implementation. Solutions for agricultural production require give-and-take at the ground level. Very seldom will one size "fit all" across the landscape of our farming culture. In addition, these compromises require a reasonable time frame to be agreed upon and implemented. This is something most people outside of agriculture simply don't understand.

How can agriculture avoid this and improve?

It comes back to how honest we are with ourselves, and how we communicate this honesty within the agricultural community. Only after this step has been accomplished should we communicate openly in the larger public debate. The process starts by engaging in the conversation internally, away from the bright lights of the press and media. To believe that we can effectively represent a quality position to the larger public, without this internal discussion, will make it only that much more challenging.

When it's time to go public, I'm an advocate for bringing people with diverse views and opinions together. Ideally, the group selected for the task will work primarily with facts – although personal viewpoints are instructive to help find facts, and they really can't be avoided. Then, with facts as the guideposts, we engage in conversation. This conversation may require a significant period of time in order to thoroughly explore the options. This is also the moment when emotion and attitudes can, and will, emerge. Ignoring them will only cause people to become angry, or even leave the process without a resolution.

One begins the resolution process by seeking new knowledge – new facts or a different way to look at an issue that could potentially provide solutions. This will initiate new understanding. When understanding happens, it is a very natural human response for there to also be a shift in one's attitude – the very thing that drives human behavior. This process, properly done, will allow all who are involved to be exposed to new thinking. In a well-managed process where acceptance is the rule, the likelihood of progress is substantially improved. To blindly defend the status quo – absent new information and knowledge – while increasing negativity, exchanging barbs intended to encourage anger, or expressing arrogance that devalues others will not obtain the results that agriculture must have to continue doing what we have been entrusted to accomplish.

This is a cultural reorientation. If you look at the continuum from beginning to end, there is a gradual cultural shift towards addressing any present difficulties of modern agriculture that are likely to provoke negative public exposure. If we refuse to make a shift, and a problem becomes such that it affects the common good of others in society, someone else (and not an individual friendly to our position) is going to make decisions about our lives and our businesses. My experience clearly demonstrates that it's very unlikely we will appreciate their decision. I have witnessed a long history of these occurrences during the 30 years I have been involved in public policy.

What are some examples?

There are many. Currently, we are confronting some persistent water-quality issues related primarily to how farmland is being managed. Some farmers are doing well on this front, yet quite a few are ignoring the evidence around the issue and, as a result, continue to contribute to the problem. For example, Iowa recently received 3–4+ inches of rainfall in a very short period of time. This happens a couple times a year, and is not just limited to this state. From my travels across Iowa on numerous occasions, it becomes apparent that there is a lot of, what I call, 'recreational' tillage occurring every year – especially this last fall, as farmers finished harvest early and had ample time to till the land.

The problem is that these lands should have never been touched post-harvest. So much of Iowa farmland is easily capable of being no-till in the spring. The slope in a fair portion of the state is steep enough that water moves very quickly off the land to waterways and eventually to the river. By not tilling and leaving the crop residue on the surface, rapid water runoff carrying soil particles is substantially reduced. It has been proven over and over by present-day research in a number of institutions. Rather than tilling, the responsible decision for farmers is to use their time and machinery resources to plant a cover crop to protect the soil surface even more.

In Des Moines, the city's water facility has filed a lawsuit against farmers who operate in their watershed. I'm certain that those water authorities are frequently collecting data that demonstrates increased nitrogen and phosphorus levels, as well as high levels of sediment. Removing soil particles is easier, but to mitigate soluble phosphorus and nitrogen in drinking water is a far more expensive technology. Should we allow that to happen if it can be prevented at the farm level? What would we do if we were a member of the non-farming public paying a higher water bill to have these nutrients removed? What would be our response if we didn't farm and experienced these higher rates due to a problem which originated on farmland upstream? These are the kinds of questions that need to be addressed by honestly asking difficult questions of ourselves, internally, before the issue gets out into the general media and/or – as has happened more frequently of late – the court system. With water quality, we are already exposed and I believe we will now pay a price for waiting to address the issue. However, we can do better on some of the other issues that are just emerging.

Unquestionably, agriculture would be best served by getting out in front of these concerns well before the activists and urban media reporters show up to ask the questions.

Some complaints about farming are simply frivolous and/or represent a legitimate compromise of farmers growing abundant food supplies. Yet some issues can, and must, be addressed if we are to be responsible in our part of life on this planet.

9

TURNING UP THE VOLUME ON SCIENCE

> Some deep questions have been raised in our society that affect all of us, and the contribution of scientists to that discussion is vital … It has probably never been more important for the public to understand science.[1]
>
> *(Alan Alda)*

Perceptions of agriculture differ. Emotions on food run high. Science, the quest for knowledge of our physical or material world gained through objective observation and experimentation, is the steadying force in this unsteady world. It clears confusion, answers questions, and matter-of-factly presents alternatives and consequences to complex issues. We rely on science every day to interpret intricate information and provide solutions. Yet due to the specialization required in science, and the rigorous training involved, it falls upon a subset of our population to perform this critical work. Due to the selective nature of the profession, and the small amount of society in the field, there isn't easy or instant access for everyone to the findings of science. The important messages of science need to reach the broader public, but they frequently don't.

In this chapter, we look at the role of academics in providing science-based research. Academics are incredibly critical to any dialogue, not just in food and agriculture. They know *a lot* of very detailed information about a vast array of important issues. On nearly any question you can imagine, there are academics out there seeking a research-based answer. Often they have figured out a way to measure it, model it, or simulate it that will either yield an answer, or at least rule out one particular scenario. Academics build on an existing body of knowledge and in some cases challenge, or even completely break down, what had been previously accepted.

Academics, as in any other profession, vary in their style, approach, and depth of expertise. Some may take one particular element of one particular issue and delve into it deeply, more deeply than most of us can even imagine. They may dedicate their entire lives to understanding one tiny microcosm of an issue we have never considered; for example, how a pig embryo regulates the structure of its DNA or perhaps amino acid lysine antitrust litigation. One of our interviewees referred to this as 'bench science' – cutting-edge stuff where the benefits aren't as broad or readily obvious, but important just the same, as it pushes the boundaries of our knowledge and can propel us into the future. Other academics may have a deep understanding of a whole host of issues under the umbrella of a larger issue.

Yet this extremely high-level, specialized mental exercise does not guarantee skilled communication, or at least not the kind that can be easily consumed by the public. Researchers and academics are not generally trained to communicate with the public, nor do they study communication unless it happens to be their particular field. It is wrong to assume that simply because an academic or researcher has demonstrated intelligence they understand the fundamentals of effective communication.

Agricultural academics in specific are a diverse lot, and it's difficult to lump them together. First of all, the range of areas an academic in agriculture studies varies dramatically – from the many uses of fiber in hemp to the economic potential of second-generation biofuels. In addition, each appointment and institution is unique and so is their level of outreach. Generally speaking, agricultural academia is broken down into three parts: research, teaching, and outreach. The outreach element of agricultural academia is what sets those working in it apart from so many other academic areas (and even each other, as we will see). To understand this requires a look at some history.

Land grant universities grew out of the Morrill Act of 1862. Congress established this system at the height of the US Civil War when it literally granted land to states (hence the name 'land grant') for institutions of higher learning.[2] These institutions were meant to promote practical education of the 'industrial classes.' Simply put, Congress gave land and money to create universities to make education of practical, useful matters available to more than just the wealthy and the elite. Agriculture was one of those practical areas of study. From here grew the roots of teaching and researching agricultural matters.

The outreach element came later and is tied to the Smith–Lever Act of 1914. This act created what is now known as Agricultural Extension. Extension was intended to help farmers learn new agricultural techniques.[3] Back then, it was hard for these rural farmers to come by education. Extension made a huge impact in helping them learn new techniques and develop rural communities. Extension services were connected to land grant universities. This is how agricultural academics came to play such a major role in outreach to farmers and rural communities.

Extension services still exist, but funding has been in decline and in some states there is no longer a local presence. So while some states, like Indiana, have Extension educators in every county, other states no longer have Extension professionals embedded in communities. For example, Purdue University is a land grant university, and due to the high presence of Extension educators in Indiana, Purdue agricultural academics are able to easily outreach to farmers and rural communities through this local presence. It can be as easy as shooting an email to a listserv of Extension staff members.

For those agricultural academics who live in states without strong Extension services, outreach is a much greater challenge. In addition, back in 1914 when Extension was established, many Americans really needed it. It was highly valued because it was hard to get information and a higher percentage of the population worked in agriculture. Today, few outside of agriculture have heard of Extension.

Keeping this in mind, agricultural academics have a tendency towards outreach that is stronger than some other academic areas based on the Extension mission. However, with the decline in Extension funding and the variance between states, it is impossible to categorize all academics into one set. In addition to all of this, Extension was intended to create a line of communication and outreach to farmers and rural communities – not consumers at large. Today, Extension runs the risk of neglecting the vast majority of the public and the additional challenge of staying relevant to the changing needs of our population.

Extension outreach is valuable, but it is in decline and it is only known to a narrow swath of the population. With this background and context, there are three challenges to communication around food and agriculture that academics face. First, there is a lack of incentive and urgency to communicate with the community at large. Second, academic work is complex and particular, which leads to jargon-speak that is alienating to the public. Third, academics are neutral (meaning they don't take sides on heated issues and they let their science speak for itself). These three matters block a frustrating amount of critical information from reaching the four other players – consumers, farmers, agribusiness, and policymakers.

Imagine the following. It's a Tuesday during fall semester and Professor Jane is up to her eyebrows. She quickly runs through her priorities. She has a class tomorrow at 10:30 am that she needs to prep for. There's a research grant due next week on Monday. The deadline to submit her journal paper to a conference is in less than two weeks. When her review committee meets at the end of the semester to assess whether she gets promoted, they are going to look at how much she's published, what kind of grant money she pulled in, and maybe her teaching evaluations.

Jane knows that communicating with the public is important and valuable, but it's not a priority. For many professors, communication with the public is not a part of their job descriptions. It is encouraged in Jane's case but it continually slips off her radar because the rewards aren't clear or well supported. As the system currently exists, she has little time to share her knowledge with the general public. In order to stay on the cutting edge in her field, she also must spend a lot of time reading, researching, and keeping up to date with the many complexities of the academic microcosm she calls home. This involves a considerable amount of time spent alone in her small office.

In the process of writing and researching for this book, we spoke with a number of academics in the field of agriculture. One of the many to generously share their time was Dr. Otto Doering. With decades of experience under his belt, he is intimately acquainted with the ins and outs of the agricultural policy world. The nature of his work is interacting with policymakers and this has taught him many informal but extremely important lessons on communication. During our interview, he told us how often he had seen missed communication opportunities between academics and outside groups. He gave us an example: "I watched an economist stand up in front of an important decision-making group and go through equations and everyone's eyes just rolled up. That's just not the way to deal with that. But economists will do that and it's death. You're dead meat the minute you do that."

Communicating with policymakers means taking an academic message and parsing it down into understandable English with clear indications of why something matters *now* and what the implications are. This academic he was speaking of? We will refer to him as John. John's chances of communicating with that audience were diminished. An invaluable opportunity to educate decision-makers on facts that could sway their stances was gone. John was irrelevant to that audience, but neither his paycheck nor his academic standing would take a hit because of a mediocre presentation.

John will continue doing his research, publishing journal articles, writing grants for funding, teaching, getting promoted, and getting paid. The reason he will forge ahead as usual is because those are the things he is rewarded for. John is following the path he knows he has to follow for success. He spent almost ten years on a salary that barely afforded him even ramen noodles for dinner to obtain his PhD at long last, and he wouldn't mind getting a nice salary now.

When you've struggled for years like John in order to the get the prestigious 'Dr.' in front of your name, making somewhere between $10,000 and $20,000 a year while watching your friends go on to things like *homeownership and children*, you follow the incentives path that is laid out in front of you. The whole scenario is a major catch-22. We all deserve better science communication surrounding food and agriculture, but we're giving those who can do it little incentive. Some do so out of a personal interest or because they believe it is the right thing to do. Yet in an extremely competitive environment like research, there's very little time to follow the public-spirited route just because you think you should. It is a systemic issue, and the importance of a strong, scientific voice looking out for the best interest of farmers and consumers is too important to leave to 'spare time' and an altruistic drive.

The second matter is the use of jargon. An example would be if you asked an agricultural economist what they did, and they responded, "Oh, my research is to identify the minimum subsidy that would induce a risk-neutral rotation corn and soybean farmer to adopt no till in a silty clay loam, poorly drained soil type given past and future weather variability and corn prices."

Any reader outside of a tiny subset of agricultural economists likely experienced frustration before even completing the sentence. It doesn't sound relevant or important to their life. The thing is, though, it *is* important. Basically, no till means that you don't plow. It is better for soil health, offsite erosion, and nutrient runoff. What this academic is trying to find out is how we can give farmers a good reason not to plow their land and leave the previous stalks in place to protect the soil. It's an environment-saving practice.

Nicholas Kristoff of *The New York Times* wrote about this recently in an op-ed entitled, "Professors, We Need You!" "A basic challenge is that Ph.D. programs have fostered a culture that glorifies arcane unintelligibility while disdaining impact and audience," he writes, rather stingingly. "A related problem is that academics seeking tenure must encode their insights into turgid prose. As a double protection against public consumption, this gobbledygook is then sometimes hidden in obscure journals – or published by university presses whose reputations for soporifics keep readers at a distance."[4]

Jargon induces frustration, and Kristoff's words sound a lot like those of a frustrated man. It isn't just consumers at large who feel this. Don Villwock, President of the Indiana Farm Bureau, told us, "The scientific research university folks are guilty of talking to themselves and talking in complex words. When you communicate with the public, you're supposed to communicate at the sixth or eighth grade level. That's a complete disconnect for university folks. I have been a proponent for a long time, especially at Purdue, that all the research teams need to have an Ag Communicator on board. A lot of things they do are the best-kept secret. They will publish in a journal and do all the things that they have to do to get tenure and get promoted."

There are researchers themselves who are well aware of it. Dr. Allan Gray, professor at Purdue University and Director of the Center for Food and Agricultural Business, explained it like this: "You're writing a master's thesis. Who are you writing that for? Frankly, you're writing it for the university faculty. That's the natural place we start from – writing for other academics. The style we learn to write in is to prove to somebody else that we know what we're talking about. With our stakeholder audiences, it's rarely the case that we need to prove that we know what we're talking about. They take that at face value."

From day one in academic and research training, students are taught to write and communicate to other academics. It's a culture. It's an environment. Gray said, "What we need to answer are three really important questions about the research that we need to communicate to non-academic stakeholders: So what? Who cares? Why would they care? For a lot of us, this is really hard to do. Our writing is for academics and the purpose for our research is for the edification of ourselves and a set of colleagues that we work with."

So why do academics speak and write this way? Precision, environment, and habit. In academia you are rewarded for accuracy, and often complex jargon becomes the most precise way to capture a concept. This compounds itself due to environment. Surrounded by a niche of people who do what you do, it's common to use these terms regularly, and they can often become increasingly complex and even "code word" in nature. Finally, over a period of time, it becomes habit, and to cease speaking and communicating in this way becomes a challenge.

The third challenge is neutrality. Why is this a challenge? Because neutral can be frustrating and doesn't make for a good entertainment factor. Yet it is an extremely important contribution. The burden is on everyone else – consumers, farmers, agribusiness, and policymakers – to internalize and understand this. Academics are not advocates. They don't take sides. Gray explained, "What are we really good at? We're really good at alternatives and consequences. There are some folks that don't like that very much. They think that we're not helping at all because we are neutral ground and they want us to take a position."

This poses a challenge in today's communication world. Dr. Jill Lepore, professor at Harvard University and staff writer for the *New Yorker*, wrote: "In an online culture that values opinion and personality over research and reporting, academics keen to reach readers generally have the best shot at success if they are willing to offer cavalier and often unsubstantiated opinions, promote their own work, and even expose their lives to public view." It's blunt but true. "Peer review may reward opacity, but a search engine rewards nothing so much as outrageousness."[5]

While we can encourage more and clearer communication from our scientists, what makes their voices so crucial is their neutrality. It is short-sighted to wish them to take a side on any particular matter. Scientific results should be free from agenda, advocacy, and outrageousness. "The part of our agricultural system that is most envious to the rest of the world deals with our agricultural research ... Our innovation and technology on our farms and ranches is absolutely unprecedented anywhere else. It's a marvelous system and at the core of it is publicly-funded, basic research," said Chuck Conner, former US Deputy Secretary of Agriculture.

Notes

1   Alan Alda Center for Communicating Science™ (n.d.). Retrieved January 8, 2016, from http://www.centerforcommunicatingscience. org/.

2   "Primary Documents in American History," *Morrill Act: Primary Documents of American History (Virtual Programs & Services, Library of Congress)*. Web. 17 November 2015. https://www.loc.gov/rr/ program/bib/ourdocs/Morrill.html.

3   "Smith–Lever Act," *Special Collections Research Center: Green 'n' Growing*. Web. 17 November 2015. https://www.lib.ncsu.edu/special collections/greenngrowing/essay_smith_lever.html.

4   N. Kristof (2014, February 15) "Professors, We Need You!" Retrieved November 3, 2015, from http://www.nytimes.com/2014/02/16/ opinion/sunday/kristof-professors-we-need-you.html?_r=0.

5   J. Lepore (2013, September 3) "The New Economy of Letters." Retrieved November 5, 2015, from http://chronicle.com/article/ The-New-Economy-of-Letters/141291/.

An academic's perspective on ...

THE COSTS OF NOT SPENDING

Dr. Ken Foster is a professor and the head of the Department of Agricultural Economics at Purdue University.

"Negative growth" – the ultimate oxymoron of economics – epitomizes publicly funded agricultural research and extension since the 1990s.[1] The result of this decline is multifaceted. For one, tuition rates have soared in order to support the activities of universities that train students to push the frontiers of their disciplines.

In addition, basic trust in academic agricultural scientists' discoveries has eroded because they struggle to respond in a timely fashion on important issues. Why? Partially a lack of public support, and partially the result of this – scientists having to form partnerships with industry in order to fund research efforts. The latter point is *extremely* sensitive because it questions the integrity of the research process. That is, can academic research that is dependent on private funding support be truly unbiased ... and will university professors feel free to pursue research that is viewed as controversial by industry?

Regardless of the actual answer to this question, the fact that it is raised means that uncertainty exists, and this uncertainty erodes the trust in science as the answer to fundamental questions about food production and processing.

The rate of return on public support for agricultural research and development is crucial in this debate, yet largely goes ignored. In a recent and detailed study,[2] a group of academics measured the impact of state-level investments in agricultural research and extension in the 48 contiguous US states from 1949 to 2002. Their results were telling. For *every* dollar invested, there was a country-wide return of between

$10 and $70, with a mean of $32. This means that every dollar spent on research has a national return of, on average, $32. This clearly suggests that additional public resources could have been devoted to agricultural R&D, with substantial beneficial return.

While private research and development in agriculture also has high monetary returns, it is focused on generating profits for agribusinesses and other private-sector participants – typically not farmers. Agribusinesses are in the business of selling agricultural inputs (seed, fertilizer, agro-chemicals, etc.) and therefore are unlikely to invest in low-input agriculture or innovations where the monetary benefits accrue to farmers. Most private-sector R&D advances in agriculture are adopted by farmers as a matter of staying competitive with other farmers and not gaining additional profit.

This is, in essence, the crux of the public debate in the food and agricultural sector. Consumers are generally interested in sustainability, local production, and organic food (driven in large part by a desire for low-input food production). But agribusinesses have a core competency in the development and marketing of production inputs, and they are the ones increasingly funding agricultural research and capturing the benefits.

Public institutions undertaking agricultural research today are much more likely to be responsive to longer-term social interests because their funding sources are less directly linked to the short-term demands of private-sector shareholders to create value. In other words, research at universities is not a "for profit" industry – our results don't have to produce money for shareholders, but rather value for society.

Dr. Julian Alston, a professor of agricultural and resource economics at UC Davis, has reviewed studies[3] that conclude that public research can take decades to generate its full value. That's a long time to wait for results, although the results are well worth waiting for. The irony is that the general public's election of representatives who cut public support for land grant research universities has likely undermined their desire for more science focused on low-input sustainable practices.

It is likely that vocal elements on both sides of the debate misrepresent the interests and values of the other. It is also likely that those who are genuine in their points of view, regardless of which "camp" they inhabit, have more in common than not. That is, the farmer who toils to feed others while making a comparatively good living has no interest in polluting the environment or using more inputs than necessary to achieve her goals. Likewise, the consumer who desires a wholesome, safe, and environmentally sustainable diet has no interest in impoverishing farmers. Both desire a safe, sustainable, low-cost source of nutritious food in the market-place. The farmer hopes her children will carry on the tradition of farming and to do so needs to maintain the integrity of the land and environment. The consumer hopes to feed her family wholesomely and leave them with a clearer picture of prosperity and quality of life.

A successful communication strategy for the industry requires focus on these common values. Once the common values are established, and all agree to look to science to answer remaining questions, an agenda for public research can be established with broad support from the electorate. This public support can be directed to address pressing problems and understanding the definitive science underlying remaining disagreements. We know, based on existing data analyses, that the payoff to such an approach for society will be extremely high.

Notes

1   Y. Jin and W. Huffman (2013) "Reduced U.S. Funding of Public Agricultural Research and Extension Risks Lowering Future Agricultural Productivity Growth Prospects," Working Paper No. 13019, Department of Economics, Iowa State University, Ames, IA.

2   J. Alston, M. Andersen, J. James, and P. Pardey (2010) *Persistence Pays: U.S. Agricultural Productivity Growth and the Benefits of Public R&D Spending*, New York: Springer.
3   J. Alston (2010) "The Benefits of Agricultural Research and Development, Innovation, and Productivity Growth," OECD Food, Agriculture, and Fisheries Papers, No. 31, OECD Publishing.

PART III
A reorientation

We have seen in Part I and Part II that all stakeholders in food and agriculture – consumers, farmers, researchers, policymakers, and agribusiness – face challenges when communication fails. To prevent these failures and realize our potential, all five players must be willing to contribute to the solution. Part III presents a reorientation in our approach to the agricultural dialogue that focuses on a true recognition of the importance of communication, the strength in a diversity of perspectives, and the ability to see common ground in an environment of heightened polarization.

10

WORKING WITH, NOT AGAINST

The power of a diversity of perspectives

As children, we assume that everyone lives in a world like ours. We have no frame of reference and no experience. We only know what we have personally seen and lived. We transpose our experiences onto everyone else and assume they believe what we believe and live the way we live. Over time, as we are exposed to different people and situations, we broaden our horizons and expand our understanding of life.

As adults, we must consider other points of view, although it takes effort and hard work to place ourselves in another person's shoes. When we disagree with someone, it can be much harder work than we like to admit to see it 'through their eyes.' In many cases, we may just shut down and walk away. We develop excuses to justify this stance. "They don't know what they're talking about." "I can't trust them." "I don't have the time." "They're just out to get me." "My way is best."

In many iterations and forms, there is a lot of this in the dialogue around food and agriculture. Although our excuses for shutting ourselves off against other perspectives feel justifiable, in the end they are merely a proxy for a belief that our feelings and experiences are more valuable than someone else's. This type of closed approach inhibits true communication – a practice that starts with listening and understanding.

Inclusive processes have been proven time and again to deliver better and more effective results. We can recognize the value in having these five different players – farmers, consumers, researchers, policymakers, and agribusiness – in our dialogues. We can create more open and effective communication if we orient ourselves towards this belief. Each party can take the same steps towards initiating an appreciation of the diversity of perspectives in this field.

Diversity creates strength. There is a wide breadth of literature on this subject, but an article by Katherine W. Phillips, Professor of Leadership and Ethics at Columbia University, drives the point home. In "How Diversity Makes Us Smarter," Phillips explains that members of a homogenous group rest assured they will agree with one another, so they prepare less. However, when people confront a diverse group, they not only prepare better but work harder cognitively and socially. "The pain associated with diversity can be thought of as the pain of exercise. You have to push yourself to grow your muscles. The pain, as the old saw goes, produces the gain. In just the same way, we need diversity – in teams, organizations and society as a whole – if we are to change, grow and innovate."[1]

Differing perspectives have value. Dr. Janet Ayres, sociologist for many years in Purdue's Department of Agricultural Economics, dedicated her career to facilitating difficult conversations and conflicts. In her much-beloved trainings, she said, "One of the first things I always say about communication is to remember we are human and with that humanness comes a couple of things. One, each of us needs to be valued and respected by others. As we are communicating with others, we need to always keep in mind to respect. Also, each of us is unique."[2] It can be very difficult to maintain respect and appreciation for different perspectives when confronted with controversial issues. This is when emotions come into play. "We're uncomfortable with emotions – all of us. In terms of our own emotions, we often don't know how to handle them. We don't know what to do when others are emotional," Dr. Ayres explains, "Our challenge isn't to deny the emotions, but to learn how to manage our own emotions."[3]

Challenge our beliefs. Is what we know "right"? Or is it possible that we don't have the full story? Dr. Kathryn Sorrells writes about this in the context of globalization and our intercultural challenges, yet her approach also applies quite well to the different players in food and agriculture. She identifies the first step as 'inquiry.' She writes, "Curious inquiry about those who are different from ourselves leads us to engagement with others. While it may sound simple, inquiry also requires that we are willing to take risks, allow our own way of viewing and being in the world to be challenged and perhaps changed, and that we are willing to suspend judgments about others in order to see and interpret others and the world from different points of view."[4]

To truly appreciate a diversity of perspectives, we might need to think about how we can incentivize the facilitation of better understanding and communications around agriculture. Incentives in education aren't always there. In the meantime, as individuals we can make a genuine effort to go out of our way to interact with those who are different. Farmers can seek out consumers, researchers can seek out policymakers, and so on and so forth. Rather than questioning the credibility of a different group of people sight unseen, we can go the extra mile to interact with someone first. This means making the time and embracing the fact that we might feel a little bit uncomfortable along the way.

The field of food and agriculture is uniquely challenging in this regard not only because the field itself is complex, but because there are complex moral dilemmas involved in many of the issues – and we live in a time of polarized politics. Debates are stark and oversimplified, while solutions to current problems in food production and agriculture are complicated. For example, sustainability and production are often viewed as mutually exclusive – it can only be one or the other. Yet both are necessary elements for a successful path forward.

Dr. Fred Whitford, botany and plant pathology expert, finds himself frustrated by the starkness of the debate and how it makes decision-making so much more difficult in the agricultural world. "How we do we protect both production and environment? That's not the message that we often hear. At the national level – it seems like there is this either/or, black or white. And there is no such thing as this notion in agriculture. It's not like abortion or gay rights where it is an either/or proposition." It's difficult to envision a world where an ensemble of business models could work. Looking at these issues it's easier to say it should be one way or another. Just as a diversity of perspectives need to be heard, it may be that a hybrid of business models could work for us.

GMOs are yet another example, one that we have looked at in depth in this book. Part of the reason we come to different conclusions is because we hold different worldviews, moral judgments, and intuitions about the way food should be. Differences in culture have also helped explain why acceptance varies from country to country. On both sides we see a moral issue: on one side, the ethics of altering genetics; on the other, concern about depriving developing countries of food security.

There is a small segment of the population that is loud and polarizing. It's unlikely that improved communications will change their perspective on agriculture from one based on perception to one based on fact. There is a small percentage of people who will never open themselves up to a diversity of perspective. However, this is by far the minority – and they should not be allowed to dictate the course of our dialogues or dissuade us from communications efforts.

Diversity of perspectives is crucial. And so is recognizing the value of communication enough that we take the necessary steps to overcome the discomfort of facing diverse viewpoints. In our final chapter, Chapter 11, we focus on a helpful tool for easing the path forward, one that can frame many conversations on food and agriculture across a wide array of players.

Notes

1   Katherine W. Phillips (2014, October 1) "How Diversity Makes Us Smarter." *Scientific American*. Scientific American, 1 October 2014. Web. 15 December 2015. http://www.scientificamerican.com/article/how-diversity-makes-us-smarter/.

2   J. Ayres (2015, March 25) "Leadership Video Series: Interpersonal Communication." Retrieved December 15, 2015, from https://www.youtube.com/watch?v=5bTUMpKDdSU.

3   J. Ayres (2015, March 25) "Leadership Video Series: Controversial Public Issues." Retrieved December 15, 2015, from https://www.youtube.com/watch?v=DlnTyGap5fw.

4   Kathryn Sorrells (2013) *Intercultural Communication: Globalization and Social Justice*, Thousand Oaks, CA: Sage.

11

SETTLING INTO COMMON GROUND

The future of food and agriculture

How do you measure the value of a carefully worded, thoughtful speech on an agricultural issue? What kind of economic return do you get from taking the time to create education tools for the general public? How do you count the value of compromise and the painstaking process of communication necessary to get there?

Communication is notoriously difficult to measure. You can put a dollar amount on a sale, a number on how many tomatoes are produced, and a weight on the number of pounds you see on the scale. Inches of rain over the last ten years can be averaged and the number of journal articles that were published can be listed on a resume.

Yet for the vast majority of communication efforts, you will never see tangible, measurable results of your labor. Communicators are often keen on social media and Google analytics because there is finally something to show, and that is a great relief to communications specialists who feel constant pressure to justify their labor. "We were retweeted three times!" "There have been 342 visitors to our website over the past week!"

However, from everything we have seen in these past pages, we know that the most powerful and effective communication on tough, nuanced issues does not occur from a tweet or a website visit (although these are valuable communication tools in their own right – and can lead someone towards good information). The best communication happens when we listen, understand, and then respond from a thoughtful place. One meaningful conversation with one single person on the complexities of GMOs can have ramifications far beyond a recipe for bacon-wrapped hotdogs that was retweeted 14 times. One carefully prepared, in-person presentation for a group of ten people can mean more than a year's worth of newsletters. Yet how do you present this value to an executive committee or stakeholders demanding to see a return? Therein lies the crux of the matter.

We can almost never know when our communication efforts have planted an idea in someone's head that completely alters their viewpoint and behavior. Some people don't internalize what has been said and continue on as normal. Others won't immediately respond or appear to understand, but reflect on it later and slowly change their thought process. A few instantly alter their views. They rarely provide feedback, and if they do, it's hardly anything that can be quantified in a spreadsheet.

We can all surely remember a time that someone said something to us, or took the time to explain something, that completely altered the way we saw the world and our place in it. Most of the time, the person delivering this message didn't know that those select words – written or spoken – carried such a powerful weight. Yet those moments when someone took the time to explain something to us, or kindly correct a misconception, can live with us forever.

On the last day of class, I ask my students to share with their classmates the most powerful thing they learned that semester. I am always surprised that something I said only once, or something I said that wasn't directly related to course material, inevitably gets mentioned. One time a student told me that my reassurance that she would have friends once she left college changed her outlook for her professional life. Another actually remarked that my comment that we should not worry about what we wear, but who we are, would stick with her forever.

These 'communications' weren't related to my subject course matter, they were never going to be on a test, and were presented on no PowerPoint – yet my comments were sincere and were in response to the concerns that I heard from my students. I did not downplay their feelings and worries and I didn't assume that they knew these things already. They are young, inexperienced, and concerned.

Are these types of 'communications' something that one can measure and put economic value on? This is one of the greatest challenges confronting communication. The best of it is not measurable. In today's world, that which is not measurable can often mean that which is not perceived to be valuable. We need to justify what we do, and if we can't measure it how do we justify it?

Despite the intangible nature of communication, the ramifications are quite serious. Agriculture is a system just like any other, and feedback from consumers can make it stronger. Yet agriculture and the food system should not be demonized because of misconceptions. As we saw in Part I, there is an abundance of examples of communication impacting agriculture. From a media frenzy over a misconstrued concept to a blogger's attempt to explain health in an attention-grabbing way, the repercussions for the food and agricultural sector are serious and real.

The reason we included an entire section of 'real-world examples' was largely because of the suspicious nature with which communication is viewed due to its 'immeasurability.' We wanted to offer hard proof of its importance and relevance, because those who we need the most in this dialogue are those who aren't talking – or more importantly, aren't listening.

This book is not about defending one group, or condemning another. It is about recognizing that there is a pervasive problem in our current agricultural dialogue. Agriculture, neither glamorous nor prone to catchy soundbites, is so deeply important to every human on this planet. That we should not reach our potential, or, even worse, that we should fail to feed our growing world because of a *communication problem*, is simply not something we can allow to pass. Remarkable strides have been made to create a more productive agricultural system, and we can forge a path of compromise between conflicting agendas if we take the time to realize that they might not be so conflicting after all.

We must each take responsibility for recognizing the emotions we bring to the table, our perceptions, the reality of farming today, and the possible limits of our own knowledge before jumping to a conclusion. We must hold ourselves individually accountable. This will not stop the media from starting a media frenzy, or a blogger from sharing unfounded claims. Yet every single person has the power to influence the dialogue around food and agriculture, although the exact manner of communication and the situation may differ. Farmers, consumers, agribusiness, policymakers, and researchers all have the means to communicate powerfully and effectively. Yet it requires personal responsibility. Are you sharing facts? Are you listening to concerns? Are you making the extra effort to speak in a way people will understand?

Great challenges lie ahead for our world's food and agricultural system. The world's population, at seven billion people today, is expected to exceed ten billion by the end of the century.[1] Much of this expansion will happen in urban areas, where people buy food not grow it.[2] Water scarcity and climate variability add to this challenge. Improving nutrition and public health, as well as strengthening farms and communities, are also critical challenges.[3] Excellent communication alone will certainly not solve these problems. It is, however, an important variable in the equation.

The concept of 'common ground' is gaining momentum in today's conversations about food and agriculture. Many of our interviewees referred to it as the solution to the contention and polarization in our food and agriculture dialogues. Common ground is, by definition, a basis of mutual interest or agreement.

While it sounds simple, in practice it can mean an entire reorientation of thought. Focusing on common ground is breaking the habit of honing in on what makes us different and focusing on our mutual goals. The practice of finding 'common ground' is used in many fields; mediation, advocacy, multiculturalism, psychiatry, and more.

The concept itself is broad and quite general, but in the context of communication around food and agriculture 'common ground' is being applied with a very specific purpose. The purpose is to help those without agricultural backgrounds and those with agricultural backgrounds to better understand one another, and to view each other with less hostility and suspicion. In a nutshell, it pushes the fact that we have more in common with each other than we think, and we need to recognize that before jumping to conclusions about each other.

Compromise is the future of the food and agriculture debate. Whether it is in regards to animal welfare, environmental practices, organic vs. nonorganic, GMOs, or the myriad of other complex issues confronting this field, no one party is going to have it all 'their way' and, in the end, compromise generally ends up yielding a good result for such a diverse society and world. To reach compromise almost always requires belabored communication. In this context, 'common ground' practices can be used to make the process somewhat less painful. Whether you're having a dialogue with your neighbor, a scientist, a consumer, or your policymaker, when things get heated you can always calm things down and reorient the conversation by saying, "I know we both want to create a safe and sustainable food supply for our future," or "We both want our kids to be healthy and well fed," or "We both want to make sure that everyone gets enough to eat." Not only are you reminding yourself that you inevitably want the same thing, but you demonstrate to the other party that you don't want to elbow them out.

Although this example is for conversations, 'common ground' communication practices don't just stop there. Communication, as we saw in this book, happens in so many different ways. The reorientation tool of 'shared values and goals' can be utilized in a variety of media. We live in a big, diverse world and, of course, not everyone shares the same values and goals. However, you would be hard pressed to find someone you have nothing in common with around a subject as broad as food and agriculture. Go the extra mile to figure out what that is. Simply keeping this in mind while you're writing or posting on social media can shape your words and messages. It doesn't always have to be said overtly.

If you feel like you don't need this tactic, it's likely a sign that you aren't talking to the right people. No one needs to find common ground when everyone already agrees with them. Just as much as we need common ground practices in communication around food and agriculture, we need our 'five players' to boldly step outside of their comfort zone and interact with each other. The two concepts are dependent upon one another. Consumers, policymakers, researchers, agribusiness, and farmers need to work on breaking down the barriers that exist between them. Remember, the 'communication scarcity' in agriculture isn't referring to what gets said between farmer and farmer or between consumer and consumer. Quite a lot gets said in those areas. The communication scarcity refers to what gets shared (or *doesn't* get shared) between these different groups of people.

There is no way we, the coauthors of this book, can anticipate the exact types of communication situations that will arise between you, the reader, and those you interact with around these issues. In actively observing the trends, we have identified current pressure points and can anticipate what is to come. However, every communication scenario is unique, nuanced, and challenging.

In writing this book, we had to constantly remind ourselves that we were working together towards a common goal. There were many things we, your two authors, did not agree upon. We had moments of tension. However, the one thing that we *always* agreed upon was that our final product was stronger because we listened to each other and compromised. Our common value was our belief that we are damaging the future of food and agriculture by not listening enough to one another and by underestimating the power of communication. We refocused on this over and over again when disagreements arose.

If we are to create a future of agriculture that is sustainable and abundant, we need to include all of our stakeholders and cease to perceive communication as secondary in our efforts. Best of luck to each of you.

Notes

1   Bureau of Economic Analysis (2010) *GDP by Industry*, Washington, DC: BEA, US Department of Commerce.

2 R. A. Hoppe and D. E. Banker (2010) *Structure and Finances of U.S. Farms: Family Farm Report, 2010 Edition*, Washington, DC: Economic Research Service, US Department of Agriculture.
3 "Facing the Future: Critical Challenges to Food and Agriculture" (2012, May 1). Retrieved December 9, 2015, from http://www.foodandagpolicy.org/sites/default/files/Facing_the_Future_0.pdf.

APPENDIX

Additional resources on food, health, and agriculture

Government

Food and Drug Administration	http://www.fda.gov/
CDC Division of Nutrition, Physical Activity and Obesity	http://www.cdc.gov/nutrition/
ChooseMyPlate.gov	ChooseMyPlate.gov
USDA National Agricultural Library	https://fnic.nal.usda.gov/
CDC Food Safety	http://www.cdc.gov/foodsafety/
USDA Economic Research Service	http://www.ers.usda.gov/
Center on Budget and Policy Priorities	http://www.cbpp.org/
Congressional Research Service for reports on food policy	https://www.fas.org/sgp/crs/misc/RS22600.pdf

Academic

Harvard School of Health Nutrition Science	http://www.hsph.harvard.edu/nutritionsource/
Choices Magazine	http://www.choicesmagazine.org/

Groups with information on food and agriculture

Consultative Group on International Agricultural Research	http://www.cgiar.org/our-strategy/cgiar-research-programs/cgiar-research-program-on-climate-change-agriculture-and-food-security-ccafs/
International Food Policy Research Institute	http://www.ifpri.org/
AGree	http://www.foodandagpolicy.org/
The Center for Food Integrity	http://www.foodintegrity.org/
International Food Information Council (Food Insight)	http://www.foodinsight.org
Partnership for Food Safety Education	http://fightbac.org/
Chicago Council Food for Thought	http://www.thechicagocouncil.org/blog/global-food-thought
World Resources Institute	http://www.wri.org/
Earth Policy Institute	http://www.earth-policy.org/
Food Quality and Safety	http://www.foodqualityandsafety.com/

Animal welfare

American Veterinary Medical Association	https://www.avma.org/public/animalwelfare/pages/default.aspx
Temple Grandin's website	http://www.grandin.com/

Consumer groups

Consumer Federation of America	http://www.consumerfed.org/
Consumer Action	http://www.consumer-action.org/
Consumers Union	http://consumersunion.org/
National Consumers League	http://www.nclnet.org/
Center for Science in the Public Interest	http://cspinet.org/

GLOSSARY

academics
Academics are members of an institution of learning; more specifically, the people who teach and research in a college or a university. Although appointments and roles can vary, generally speaking academics (or professors) are responsible for both teaching and maintaining a vibrant research program. In agricultural programs, they often shoulder a third responsibility that centers around Extension (defined below). With rare exceptions, academics are neutral sources of information that has undergone a rigorous review process. In many cases, they are dependent upon funding to maintain their research, and as public funding for public institutions of higher learning has diminished, in recent years many must spend more time writing grants. Academics are rewarded by their institutions for rigor and discipline in their research methods, scholarly publications, grants, and in some cases for good teaching and outreach.

advocacy
Advocacy is an activity by an individual or group that aims to influence decisions within political systems, economic systems,

social systems, or institutions. Advocacy can take many forms, from media campaigns, public speaking to lobbying and more. There is a wealth of advocacy groups across the United States and the world that represent a wide array of causes. It is not uncommon for there to be multiple advocacy groups both for and against one particular issue. The advent of the internet has opened the doors to new types of advocacy that operate largely online or using social media.

agribusiness (agricultural business)

Agribusiness is the commonly used term for agricultural business. It refers to agriculture that is conducted on commercial principles. The term encompasses a range of activities and disciplines, and can include businesses that operate in the fields of breeding, crop production (farming and contract farming), distribution, farm machinery, processing, seed supply, and more. Agribusiness is a broad term that can mean slightly different things to different groups; for instance, critics of large-scale farming may use agribusiness as a negative term, whereas for other groups, such as academics of agribusiness management, it is a neutral word that refers to each of the individual elements of production and distribution. In the context of this book, we use agribusiness to refer to the agents of the food and fiber value chain.

agriculture

Agriculture is the cultivation of animals and plants for food, fiber, and other products used to sustain and enhance human life. Agriculture dates back about 10,000 years and is driven and defined by different climates, cultures, and technologies. Over the past century, agricultural practices have drastically evolved in certain places in the world (such as the United States), radically diminishing the number of people working in the field while increasing output. In the context of this book, we sometimes use 'agriculture' to refer to an umbrella group of people who are part of the agricultural community. This includes farmers, people in agribusiness, associations or other groups that represent farmers, Extension agents, and any others who consider themselves a part of the agricultural community.

animal welfare
Animal welfare is the well-being of animals. The standards of 'good' animal welfare vary considerably between different contexts. Standards are constantly being reviewed and are debated, created, and revised by animal welfare groups, legislators, and academics worldwide. Animal welfare is one of the more polarizing and sensitive topics in food and agriculture conversations. Concerns can include how animals are slaughtered for food, how they are used in scientific research, and how they are kept on farms (housing, space, the time animals spend with their young, etc.). The sensitive and emotional nature of this topic can make it one of the more difficult to debate in a productive and balanced manner.

associations
Associations are groups of individuals who voluntarily enter into an agreement to accomplish a purpose. There are associations for nearly every profession or area of interest, and many have national, state, or regional chapters. The key benefit to joining an association is to participate in a 'synergistic group' (the effect of a collection of people is greater than just one person). This can make joining an association particularly valuable to people who work in a profession that is solitary in nature. There is an array of associations that represent the interests of different groups of farmers. Most associations require that their members pay dues, and in turn provide benefits such as educational resources, networking opportunities, and more.

audience
The term 'audience' is commonly used in communications and it implies the particular demographic you are targeting with a specific message. Defining the audience is one of the initial steps in developing a communication strategy. The identity of the audience often determines the communication avenues you will use to reach them or how you might word a particular message. For example, imagine that an academic wants to convey the value of 'no till' to farmers *and* the public. These are two different audiences, and would require two different communication strategies. Farmers, for example, might respond better to messages on how this practice

won't damage their yield – whereas the public might respond better to a message on how this protects the environment.

ballot initiatives

Ballot initiatives are a form of direct democracy available in 24 states where state-level initiatives can be put on the ballot. By means of a petition signed by a certain minimum number of registered voters, a ballot initiative can bring about a public vote on a proposed statute or constitutional amendment. Ballot initiatives are also called, depending on the state, "popular initiative," "voter initiative," "citizen initiative," or just "initiative." Ballot initiatives may take the form of either the direct or indirect initiative. Under the direct initiative, a measure is put directly to a vote after being submitted by a petition. Under the indirect initiative, a measure is first referred to the legislature, and then only put to a popular vote if not enacted by the legislature.

blogger

A blogger is any person who writes, edits, and publishes a website on the internet that contains their own experiences, opinions, or insights. A blog is usually geared towards a particular audience or target audience. A blogger's goals can widely vary, but they often initiate conversation between members of their audiences. Most bloggers leave room for audience members to leave comments and raise questions about a specific topic. The rise and prevalence of bloggers has blurred the lines between opinion and fact, as many people take bloggers' posts at face value and assume the information is accurate. Bloggers, unlike many formal sources of curated information, do not have to adhere to any set standards in terms of source-checking or relaying only fact. There is a wide spectrum of bloggers, from those who write with care to those who post purely for profit (if a blogger is popular enough, they can make a living from advertisements on their blog or by agreeing to sponsor a company's product or service).

common ground

'Common ground' is a widely used term across many disciplines. At its core, it means finding a space that you can share with someone, a place both or multiple parties can occupy - hence common 'ground.' Common ground, within communications, is a technique to help facilitate communications. The basic purpose of common ground is to first seek what you have in common or share with the other, and then to focus on that over and over when confrontation or challenges may arise. It often enables parties to work together better or find compromise more easily. A focus on common goals can also ease some of the emotional elements of a conversation as it allows a person to focus less on differences, and more on reaching a decision or solution.

communication
Communication is, at the most basic level, the imparting or exchanging of information or news. In a broader context, communication is a field that centers around the two-way process of reaching mutual understanding (or not) in which participants exchange information, news, ideas, and feelings. In business, it is a key function of management within the organization, and frequently a key outreach focus to connect with stakeholders. It is also a widely studied discipline. Communication is unique in that it permeates all areas of life and all fields. Any activity that requires more than one human being is dependent upon communication, which can either hinder or help a process. Given the all-encompassing nature of the field, there are many ways to examine communication – from one-on-one interpersonal to mass media to social communication and more.

consumers
In the context of this book, we refer to 'consumers' as anyone who purchases and consumes food. Generally speaking, when we use the label of consumer, we are referring to those who do not directly participate in agricultural activities such as farming, food production, etc. – even though these portions of the population, obviously, also purchase and consume food. Consumers have become significantly more outspoken regarding their thoughts, opinions, and feelings regarding food and agriculture over the past several decades. They play a much greater role in shaping policy and influencing corporate

decision-making. The ratio of consumers to agricultural workers has shifted significantly over the past two centuries. Some two hundred years ago, the majority of our population worked in a field related to agriculture. Today, the ratio of consumer to agricultural worker is approximately 50:1. This has radically altered the way in which the communication of information occurs in this field.

diversity of perspectives
Diversity of perspectives refers to the many and varied points of view brought about through unique backgrounds, experiences, demographic segmentations, etc. of a population. Diversity of perspectives can occur between genders, religious views, social classes, races, languages, and cultures. A person's perspective is directly influenced by their immediate experiences and social factors that shape their identity. Having a diversity of perspectives is considered beneficial, in that a multitude of opinions are taken into consideration before a decision is made, and people are forced to confront a wide array of options and insights. Despite the many advantages, it is frequently challenging to manage a diversity of perspectives. It can require time, thoughtfulness, patience, tolerance, and a willingness to listen.

Extension
In the United States, 'Extension' is the commonly used name in agriculture for the Cooperative Research and Extension Services. Extension provides non-formal education and learning activities to people throughout the country: farmers, residents in rural communities, and people living in urban areas. The goal of Extension is to bring evidence-based science and modern technologies to farmers, consumers, and families. Within the United States, Extension was established by the Smith–Lever Act of 1914 as a mechanism to get information and knowledge to the public through partnerships with land grant Universities and the United States Department of Agriculture. Since the inception of Extension, this field has drastically changed, and today it varies depending on the country and state where it is located. Extension commonly provides information about agriculture and food, home

and family, the environment, community economic development, and youth and 4-H.

farmers
A farmer is a person who raises living organisms for food or raw materials. The term usually applies to people who grow crops, raise poultry or livestock, or maintain orchards or vineyards. A farmer may own the land or, in some cases, farm on rented land. Today, only a slim portion of the US population work as farmers. In this book, the term 'farmer' is used to describe the individuals who work to produce food or raw materials.

food safety
Food safety is the handling, preparation, and storage of food in order to prevent foodborne illness. This not only includes food at its origin, but also the practices of food labeling, hygiene, additives, and pesticide residue. In the United States, the Food and Drug Administration plays a large part in the regulation of food safety, including the publication of a Food Code that presents guidelines for regulating food safety within retail and food service industries. Concerns over food safety vary widely by country. The United States experiences high levels of food safety due to strong oversight and rigorous regulations, and most consumers rarely worry whether the food they eat will make them dangerously ill. Other countries' populations, with fewer regulations and less oversight, must concern themselves over food safety on a more regular basis.

global food security
Within agriculture, 'global food security' refers to the goal of obtaining food security for the world both now and in years to come. The term 'food security' relates to supply as well as access to food. It is viewed by many as the primary challenge of the global agricultural system, and a difficult one to balance given a changing climate and the world's growing population. Global food security is the creation of a strong food system worldwide that eradicates malnutrition, extreme poverty, and many diseases. Global food security is perceived to have strong economic advantages, such as

allowing governments to devote more funds to growth in other areas, including infrastructure.

GMOs (genetically modified organisms)

GMOs are organisms whose genetic structure has been modified in some way. Genetic modification encompasses cross-breeding, selective breeding, and genetic engineering (GE). Today, almost 80 percent of food in the United States is from genetically engineered crops. Through genetic engineering, these crops are modified to be drought, temperature, disease, or insect resistant. These practices have helped increase yields, limit disease and insect damage, and reduce the use of harmful pesticides and insecticides. There has been no scientific evidence that genetically modified crops are in any way more harmful or less nutritious than non-genetically modified crops.

incentives

An incentive is something that motivates a person to perform an action or behave in a particular manner. Incentives run the gamut from monetary rewards, moral standards, social pressures to personal health and more. The study and understanding of incentives is a component of economics, both in terms of individual decision-making and in terms of cooperation and competition within a larger context. In this book, we often refer to a person's or group's incentives – or lack of incentives – to communicate. Motivations to communicate in the agricultural context can vary dramatically depending on the person and their level of interest in food and agriculture, their rewards, and their goals or expected outcomes in communicating. It is critical to consider incentives when approaching a communication strategy, and to realistically assess whether the proper incentives exist amongst various communicators.

information curation

Information curation, or content curation, is the process of collecting, interpreting, and then presenting information about a particular topic. In the context of this book, we refer to information curation as the process by which information is sorted and presented to the public by various institutions. Journalists have traditionally been a major source of information curation, sorting fact from fiction and attempting to portray an objective summary of an event or issue. Other well-known 'information curators' are libraries and universities, amongst others. With the advent of the internet, there is an abundance of information that is made publicly available that has never gone through a formal process of curation. This wide availability of unsifted and unsorted information has demonstrated positive (when suppressed information is made public) and negative results (when false information is presented as true or presented without context).

jargon

Jargon is the words or terms used by a profession or group that people outside of that subset are not familiar with or find difficult to understand. Jargon arises from the use of specialized words within a field that are commonly used for precision and accuracy when sharing information. For instance, in academia, accuracy and precision in research and peer reviewed journal articles are often what makes the information so valuable. This can make it difficult to avoid jargon because more commonly understood terms may undermine some important nuances or exceptions. Yet despite these challenges, it is valuable to consider when and where jargon is being used as it can be very alienating for a general audience and can easily undermine communication efforts.

land grant colleges and universities

The land grant system began in 1862 with a piece of legislation known as the Morrill Act. The law gave states public lands – provided the lands be used to establish at least one college (hence, 'land grant' colleges) that teaches agriculture and mechanical arts. The mandate was that these land grant colleges help extend higher education to broad segments of the US population. This was in response to the growing desire and need for agricultural and technical knowledge, as well as the lack of higher education available for agricultural and industrial workers. There is at least one land grant university in each state, and these universities receive federal funding each year. A series of legislative acts endowed the colleges (many of which have grown into universities) with a three-part function encompassing teaching, research, and extension. Over the decades, the nature of demands for education and scientific pursuit changed. Today, many land grant universities are still known for their agricultural college roots – although not all.

media
Media is, collectively, the communication outlets or tools used to store and deliver information and data. It can refer to communication media or specialized communication businesses such as print media, broadcasting, publishing, photography, etc. that reach or influence people widely. It is the channel through which news, entertainment, data, or promotional messages are widely disseminated. Media is the plural of 'medium' – so it refers to several, or the collective. Today, when people refer to the 'media,' they are commonly referring to the press.

media frenzy
A media frenzy is a colloquial term that describes a news event where the media coverage is perceived to be out of proportion to the event being covered (such as number of reporters, amount of news articles being published, level of media hype). This occurs when something in the news receives massive coverage because it is considered either breaking or scandalous. A media frenzy is generally perceived to be a negative reflection on journalistic integrity, as the media gets 'swept away' in the hype of an issue and may not fact-check or rein in coverage with an objective eye. In today's world, where information can be conveyed quickly, it is easier for media frenzies to occur as outlets jump to get ahead of the story.

messaging
Messaging is a commonly used phrase in communications that refers to key, consistent points communicated to an audience. It describes how and what you communicate to a group. Different messages are developed for different purposes and for different audiences. Effective messaging uses language that resonates with the target

audience, highlights a unique value proposition or call to action, is understandable, and meets the larger goals of your organization.

mobile mind shift

The mobile mind shift is the expectation that "I can get what I want in my immediate context and moments of need." This was defined by Ted Schadler, Josh Bernoff, and Julie Ask (*The Mobile Mind Shift*, Groundswell Press, 2014). This concept refers to the change in the general public's thinking and expectations in terms of how they receive information, products, and services. This concept was developed in response to the 'immediate access' mindset provoked, in part, by the onset of smartphones. While this term is generally used in a marketing context, it also has applications to communication. There is an expectation of immediacy and easy access to information these days, and a failure to meet this can hinder the success of a communication or outreach plan.

natural

Natural refers to anything existing in or caused by nature – not made or caused by mankind. In terms of food, it is typically implied that the products are minimally processed and contain all natural products. There is a lack of standards surrounding the term and many countries provide no definition or meaning. In the United States, there are no rules or regulations for labeling or defining 'natural.'

organic

Organic refers to anything of or relating to a living organism, but in terms of agriculture organic refers to food produced by organic farming. Every country has different standards surrounding organic food; however, it generally refers to food grown without the use of synthetic pesticides or chemical fertilizers. In the United States, producers need to obtain organic certification, which serves as proof that they adhere to the rules, regulations, and government-defined standards as to what exactly classifies as organic. In addition, the United States has certain regulations for organic meat, including the type of feed, use of hormones and antibiotics, and access to pasture.

perception
Perception is the way in which a person interprets, understands, and comprehends information through one or more of his or her senses. Perception is largely a cognitive and psychological process, yet how we perceive the people and objects around us affects our communication. For example, the same message can be interpreted differently by different people. Past experience, culture, and present feelings are just some examples of the factors that shape perception. Understanding a person's outlook and background can help garner an understanding of how they may perceive certain communication attempts, and can help to narrow down what may or may not resonate with that particular person.

perception of risk
Perception of risk, a subset of perception (defined above), is how a person interprets or judges the probability and severity of a potential hazard causing some negative effect. Perception of risk can be influenced by a number of factors, including the type of risk, our ability to control our exposure to that risk, our level of knowledge about th e subject, and the influence of our peer groups. Perceptions of risk are often misaligned with the actual risks of a product, occurrence, or threat. Due to this misalignment, and the impact it can have on debates or policy, public perception of risk is increasingly recognized as an important element to consider in communication and public policy. There are many areas in agriculture that are heavily influenced by public perception of their risk (regardless of the actual risk posed), and these can range through technologies like pesticides, artificial growth hormones, genetic modification, and more.

polarization
Polarization is an increasingly common term in today's society, particularly in reference to our public political and ideological conversations. Polarization refers to the growing gap between diverging groups – and an increased disinclination to bridge that gap. This generally occurs when public opinion goes to two extremes and there is no real middle ground and no moderate

perspectives on the subject at hand (or these moderate perspectives are not being heard). As time goes by, two extremes push farther apart from one another and in turn become less willing to switch positions or reconsider their stance.

policymaker
Policymakers are responsible for making governmental policies and practices, known as public policy. Public policy is a system of laws, regulatory measures, courses of action, and funding priorities concerning a given topic disseminated by the government or its representatives. Policy is used to address problems on the local, national, or international level and can entail a number of responses, including regulations, subsidies, quotas, and laws. Some policymakers are voted into office and base many of their policies on hopes of reelection and pleasing their electorate. These elected policymakers are influenced by public opinion and sentiment.

stakeholder
Stakeholders are the people, or groups, that have an interest or concern in something. In this book, we commonly refer to agricultural stakeholders. These are the people or parties who have an interest or concern in agriculture – or particular elements of agriculture, depending on the context. Stakeholders can range from those directly involved in an operation, through investors to anyone who could help produce a positive or negative outcome around an issue. The simplest way to conceptualize a stakeholder is to imagine anyone who has a 'stake' in an issue or a field. Stakeholders can take many different shapes and forms.

transparency
Transparency is operating in such a way that it is easy for others to see what actions are being performed. It implies openness in communication and accountability. Transparency can be practiced by companies, organizations, administrations and communities, and guides an organization's policies on the disclosure of information. Transparency is highly prized in democracies, where great value is put on an individual's ability to make informed decisions. Agriculture

can face unique challenges to transparency, as access is often not easy (for example, many practices in agriculture occur far away from urban settings, making it difficult for the public to view them or participate in them).

INDEX

Locators in **bold** refer to definitions.